Agricultural Credit by Commercial Banks: Macro & Micro Analysis

Dr.E.P. Sengottuvel,

Assistant Professor,

Department of Commerce,

Gobi Arts & Science College, Gobichettipalayam.

Published by

BONFRING®
Intellectual Integrity

Agricultural Credit by Commercial Banks: Macro & Micro Analysis

9 789386 638397 >

ISBN 978-93-86638-39-7

Author

Dr.E.P. Sengottuvel

Bonfring

309, 2nd Floor, 5th Street Extension, Gandhipuram,

Coimbatore-641 012.

Tamilnadu, India.

E-mail: info@bonfring.org | Website: www.bonfring.org

Phone: 0422 4213231

Preface

India is considered as one of the emerging economy, introduced various market oriented reforms in the early 1990s which was noted as a deliberate move to liberalise the economy. In particular, financial sector came across with considerable reforms due to its contribution to the overall economic development. Until reforms, developing economies has given little importance to the role of commercial banks in economic development. Since 1990, financial liberalization has changed the operating environment of banks, by giving more flexibility to the banker in choosing their own portfolio.

Programmes of directed credit attempts to intervene in the way that banks allocate credit. Without government intervention, the bank will not allocate funds to those projects for which the social returns are the highest. Ever since the two rounds of nationalisation of major commercial banks in 1969 and 1980, directed credit has continued to be an integral part of monetary policy. The narashiman committee has recommended for phasing out of the directed credit programmes and widening the definition of credit to agriculture. In the case of India, the introduction of banking sector reforms discourages the directed credit after 1991 and widens the definition for the directed credit policies.

This main goal of this book is to examine the quantitative importance of commercial bank credit to agriculture not only at a macroeconomic level but also includes the relevant institutions such as banks and the ultimate farmers' possible interactions between them. This book believes that it gives a better insight into the relative quantitative impact of changes in bank credit in emerging economy like India where the Directed Credit Policy Prevails.

Acknowledgement

First and foremost, I owe it all to my **Satguru** for granting me the wisdom, health and strength to undertake this work task and enabling me to its successful completion of this work.

On a personal note, I am indebted and don't know to express my thanks to My **Mentor** for the overall moral support which made it possible for me to see the light of the day and to my **Parents**, my **Sisters** and my **Family members** for their patience, support and encouragement for publishing this book.

During my earlier academic days in schooling and graduation times, I used to think about doing doctorate and it was a dream for me. But today, my dream has become true because of **Research Supervisor** whose encouragement and guidance have been a source of deep and heartfelt inspiration to me.

I am grateful to the **Principal** for his encouragement, inspiration and for his interest in successfully completing this book.

I would like to express my gratitude to the many people who saw me through this book and all those who provided support, talked things over, read, wrote, offered comments, allowed me to quote their remarks and assisted in the editing, proofreading and design.

Finally, I thank the **Bonfring Publications** for publishing this book in a wonderful manner.

Dr.E.P. Sengottuvel

Chapters	Contents	Page No

CHAPTER I

INTRODUCTION AND DESIGN OF THE STUDY

1.1. Introduction

A peasant farmer saying that "abundance of water destroys life; paucity of water destroys life" signifies agriculture's link with monsoon. The vagaries of nature have been associated with ups and downs in cultivation.[1] One out of every ten people on the face of the earth lives in the Indian countryside depends directly or indirectly, on agriculture to survive. Seventy percentage of India's workforce is directly employed in agriculture, either as owner cultivators or agricultural labourers. But there are many more villagers who work in various other occupations related to agriculture. There are many women and children, who labour on their own and other's field. One begins to get a great sense of the importance of agriculture to India and its economy, and indeed to the world.[2]

India accounts for only about 2.4 percentage of the world's geographical area and 4 percentage of its water resources, but has to support about 17 percentage of the world's human population and 15 percentage of the livestock. Agriculture is an important sector of the Indian economy, accounting for 14 percentage of the nation's GDP, about 11 percentage of its exports, about half of the population still relies on agriculture as its principal source of income and it is a source of raw material for a large number of industries. Accelerating the growth of agriculture production is therefore necessary not only to achieve an overall GDP target of 8 percentage during the 12th Plan and meet the rising demand for food, but also to increase incomes of those dependent on agriculture to ensure inclusiveness.[3]

The recent Indian growth story has been service-led. Service sector has been completely replaced by agriculture, which was traditionally the largest contributor to India's GDP. However, the fact that agriculture has the smallest share in GDP of only about 14 percentage today from a high of more than 50 percentage, does not belittle its importance for the Indian economy. This is because of first, obviously, agriculture remains the single largest employer having a share of around 60 percentage. Secondly, it holds the key to creation of demand in other sectors and remains by far an important indirect contributor to India's GDP growth. The

---

[1] Srijit Mishra (2007), *"Risks, Farmers' Suicides and Agrarian Crisis in India: Is There A Way Out?"*, IGIDR Working Paper, WP-2007-014.

[2] Allen Kornmesser (1998), *"Changing Indian Agriculture: Agrarian Society, Economic Planning, and Development since 1947"*, The India Hand Book on Economic Development, Routledge, Pp. 116-119.

[3] Ministry of Agriculture (2012), *"State of Indian Agriculture 2012-13"*, GoI, New Delhi.

agriculture sector needs to grow at least by 4 percentage for the economy to grow at 9 percentage. Thus, though having a small share, the fluctuations in agricultural production can have large and significant impact on overall GDP growth. It is necessary that food prices are maintained at reasonable levels to ensure food security, especially for the deprived sections of our society. In fact, food security is emerging as an important policy concern, and the role of agriculture in ensuring equitable access to food has added a new perspective for policy makers.[1]

Agriculture and rural development are receiving considerable attention in the Developing Countries as an issue of life for a millions of rural population. India's population is predominantly rural in character with agriculture as the primary occupation. India's population is 1.21 billion by the census 2011 out of which 67 percentage are rural based. As per the economic survey of 2013 which estimates that the Indian agriculture sector contributes 14.1 percentage to the country's GDP which is considered as being a significant stakeholder. Though it contributes 14.1 percentage share of GDP, it engages 55 percentage of share of workers in the country. Besides, the agricultural sector plays a crucial role in food security of the country. [2]

With serious questions being posed regarding the food security of the country, there is a strong need, to understand the issues that plague rural agriculture credit and to address them constructively. Financial inclusion forms the corner stone of inclusive growth in any economy. However, despite having strong government regulations to direct the channel of credit to rural agricultural sectors, the financial inclusion, of the same by formal means of credit, remains abysmally low as brought out by several studies including the recent one by the Radhakrishna Committee. Lack of awareness, high risk perception, and strong presence of informal means of finance coupled with complex socio-political issues and knee-jerk reactions by governments from time to time in the event of crises have come in the way of efficient allocation of agriculture credit.[3]

Provision of adequate and timely credit at low rate of interest is one of the important inputs that can promote the well-beings of millions of small and marginal farmers by creating additional incomes and productive assets. Agricultural development is essential to overall

---

[1] Chakraborthy (2011), *"Agricultural Productivity and Credit Issues Way Forward"*, The National Seminar on Productivity in Indian Agriculture at CAB, Pune, http://rbidocs.rbi.org.in/rdocs/Speeches/ PDFs/AGP911.pdf.

[2] Mahendra Dev (2012), *"India: Roles and Challenges of Smallholders in Agriculture"*, WP-2012-014, IGIDR http://www.igidr.ac.in/pdf/publication/WP-2012-014.pdf.

[3]Abilash Nair (2010), *"Note on Improving Banks' Competitiveness while Lending to the Agriculture Sector"*, 3rd Conference on Global Competition and Competitiveness of Indian Corporate, IIM Lucknow, May 29-31.

economic progress. The main task faced by the country at the time of independence was to bring about rapid economic growth and to achieve several challenging development goals. To achieve this, the country embarked upon the strategy of five year plans for the formulation and execution of development programmes and the government started playing an important role in the creation of infrastructure for long run growth as well as the development of the agriculture sector[1].

India is considered as one of the emerging economy, introduced various market oriented reforms in the early 1990s which was noted as a deliberate move to liberalise the economy. In particular, financial sector came across with considerable reforms due to its contribution to the overall economic development. Until reforms, developing economies has given little importance to the role of commercial banks in economic development. Since 1990, financial liberalization has changed the operating environment of banks, by giving more flexibility to the banker in choosing their own portfolio.

The Indian economy continued to remain a bank based system with banks accounting for the bulk of the financial activity. The size of the banking sector in the economy tended to increase in the initial phase of development, with the increase in monetisation of the economy and thereafter declined once financial deepening sparked off a process of financial disintermediation. In the Indian case, the banking system expanded rapidly in the 1970s and 1980s after the spread of the banking network in rural areas following the nationalisation of banks in 1969. During the 1990s, the proportion of deposit growth in GDP began to plateau out as the push effect of wider of banking began to be countered by the pull effect of financial innovations such as Any Time Banking which allowed a greater churning of the same stock of money to fund a larger number of transactions. The ratio of credit to output is an indicator of financial development which continued to climb suggesting that banks remained special sources of finance in the Indian economy. Since 1990s, the Indian commercial banking sector experienced healthy growth in deposits.[2]

Banks are always referred as "backbone" for developing countries. Commercialised banks need to support various sectors to have balanced growth in the economy. In agricultural sector, small and marginal farmers suffer seriously due to non-availability of funds for their occupation. Medium and Large farmers may get necessary funds through submission of adequate collateral, while small and marginal farmers deprived of all comforts including capital

---

[1]Chand Ramesh, Raju S.S. and L.M.Pandey (2007), "Growth Crisis in Agriculture Severity and Options at National and State Levels", *Economic and Political Weekly*, 42(26), Pp. 2528-33.

[2] Ray Partha (2008), "*Commercial Banks and Monetary Policy in India*", Academic Foundation.

investment[1]. Progressive institutionalisation for providing timely and adequate credit support with particular focus on small and marginal farmers and weaker sections of the society is the call for the day – all the basic objectives of economic development namely output growth, price stability and poverty alleviation are best served by the growth of agricultural sector. But, growth in agriculture still needs credit support. At the same time, strong policy and institutional interventions were undertaken to achieve a transformation of the agricultural and rural economy. Agriculture by virtue of its size is the major determinant of employment. Farm and rural agriculture affect central and local budgets. This led to the involvement of the state in diverse activities such as procurement of large agricultural output, supply of inputs and credit, provision of subsidies of different kinds, promotion of agronomic research for adaptation of exotic varieties and development of infrastructural facilities[2].

The banking reforms did not include any specific package for agriculture. Rather, the presumption was that freeing agricultural markets and liberalising external trade in agricultural commodities would provide price incentives leading to enhanced investment and output in that sector. However, the pattern of structural adjustment and the government's macro-economic strategy since 1991 have actually been associated with a reduced rate of overall agricultural growth declines in per capital food grain output and inadequate employment generation[3]. Financial liberalisation measures, including reducing priority sector lending by banks, which have effectively reduced the availability of rural credit and thus reduced farm investment, especially by smaller farmers[4].

Initially, the reforms focused mainly on the industrial and financial sectors and agriculture was mostly kept outside the scope of reforms. However, the agricultural sector befitted indirectly from reforms due to exchange rate policy and improvements in terms of trade[5]. In a country with diverse agro-climatic, socio-economic and institutional circumstances, the need, nature and impact of input-output market reforms would differ across regions. Development of agricultural sector is critically dependent on the use of modern input such as fertilizers, seeds,

---

[1] Subramaniam and Ravi Subramaniam (2009), "Role of Banks in Agricultural lending–India".

[2] Krishnaji, N. (1990), "Agricultural Price Policy: A Survey with reference to Indian Economy", *Economic and Political Weekly*, 25(26).

[3] Chand Ramesh, Raju S.S. and L.M.Pandey (2007), "Growth Crisis in Agriculture Severity and Options at National and State Levels', *Economic and Political Weekly*, 42(26), Pp. 2528-33.

[4] Gagan Bihari Sahu (2002), *"Institutional Finance for Agriculture analysis at Macro and Micro levels"*, Unpublished Theis, ISEC, Bangalore.

[5] Dholakia Bakul H. (1997), "Impact of Economic Liberalisation on the growth on Indian Agriculture, *Agricultural Development Paradigm for the Ninth Plan under New Economic Environment*, Oxford and IBH Publishing Company, Newdelhi.

plant propagation material, agricultural chemicals and the availability of credit to purchase these and other inputs. There is a need to ensure adequate and timely supply of all these inputs.

The financial sector reforms after 1991 systematically undermined the institutional credit arrangements for agriculture. A clear and explicit reversal of the policy of social and developmental banking was the leitmotif of these reforms. However, the polity, especially since May 2004, has displayed some response to the concerns about the insufficient flow of credit to agriculture. The programme of doubling of agricultural credit in three years and provision of short-term credit to farmers at an interest rate of 7 percentage are the outcomes of these concerns. But these are basically isolated and reactive interventions aimed at improving the supply.[1]

This study aims to work the quantitative importance of commercial bank credit to agriculture not only at a macroeconomic level but also includes the relevant institutions such as banks and the ultimate farmers' possible interactions between them. This study believes that it gives a better insight into the relative quantitative impact of changes in bank credit in emerging economy like India where the Directed Credit Policy Prevails.

1.2. Statement of the Problem

In the 1970s, there was a proliferation of directed credit programs, mainly implemented in the agriculture sector throughout the world. Loanable funds were earmarked for direct availment by targeted borrowers at highly concessional rates. The funds came from three sources: government budget, special time deposits at the Central Bank, and the Central Bank's rediscounting window. Most of the loans under the directed credit programmes were extended by specialised banks, e.g., rural banks, development banks, and government financial institutions. Massive credit subsidies were provided to bring down the cost of borrowing for targeted sectors. This resulted in credit rationing of small borrowers, high default rates, and the capture of credit subsidies by large borrowers. Deposit mobilisation was also neglected due to the availability of cheap loanable funds from the government.[2]

In the case of India, the introduction of banking sector reforms discourages the directed credit after 1991 and widens the definition for the directed credit policies. If loan markets were nothing but auction markets, the interest rate would equate the demand for new funds

[1]Sathish (2011), "*Innovation in Agricultural Credit Market*", Paper presented at the International Conference 'Cracking the Nut: Overcoming Obstacles to Rural and Agricultural Finance', at Washington DC.

[2]Subbarao and Kalanidhi(1996), "*Selected Social Safety Net Programs in the Philippines: Targeting, Cost Effectiveness, and Options for Reform*", WB Discussion Papers, The World Bank, Washington, D.C.

(loans) with the supply. But credit markets are not auction markets. Rather, banking regulations give banks the right to issue money-that is, claims on goods. The bank issues these claims on the basis of its judgments concerning who is creditworthy.[1] The overall economic policy of a country has collective influence on credit supply in general for productive purposes and for agriculture in particular at different phases of policy level. Therefore, to the following questions arise:

1. What is the trend of agricultural credit by commercial banks before and after the introduction of banking sector reforms?
2. Whether Macro level variables affect agricultural credit by commercial banks?
3. Whether Bank level variables affect the agricultural credit by commercial banks?
4. Whether Micro level variables affect the agricultural credit by commercial banks?

1.3. Theoretical Review of Previous Studies

For economists, the concerns are especially important, because often rely on statistical (econometric analyses) to make inferences about what are good policies and how are working. Those inferences are only as reliable as the metrics that they are based on. Our statistical systems should tell us whether or not what are doing is sustainable, economically, environmentally, politically, or socially and whether proposed policies will in fact enhance well-being. This again proves the need of theory anything researchers discuss econometrically.[2]

There is no escape from the fact that every economist must employ a body of theory when addressing particular empirical issues. Empirist's inclined accounts which claim the primacy and objectivity of collected data as though these represent uninterpreted facts, uncontaminated judgment and theory, and as though knowledge arises from them via inductive inference, are untenable. The choice of the research question itself is the matter of the researchers' preference, and point of view. To quote " the choice of research questions, premises, the interpretation of observations, even the choice of questions to be addressed all provide scope for disagreements which evade settlement on the grounds of logic alone, even though they are transmitted or justified by reasoned argument" (Dow, 1985:35). In the choice between different theoretical specifications, empirical observations are not necessarily

[1]Stiglitz and Weiss (1990), "Banks as Social Accountants and Screening Devices and the General Theory of Credit Rationing", *Creek Economic Review,* 12, Pp. 85-118.

[2]Storm (1992), "*Macro-economic Considerations in the Choice of Agricultural Policy a study into Sectoral interdependence with reference to India*", Thesis Publishers, Amsterdam.

decisive. If they were, economic thinking would not display such a variety of ideas as it presently does and has always done.

Theoretical analyses of the interrelationships between the agricultural and non-agricultural including institutions have long history in economics, with the contributions from the Physiocrats during 17th century, from the early political economists including Ricardo, Malthus and Marx during the 19th century and from such diverse 20th century economists as Lewis, Jorgenson, Kalecki and Kaldor.[1] The ultimate objective to link the agriculture credit by institutions to agriculture is to draw policy decisions. This perspective have also touched by Keynes, Stiglitz and including Sen Amartya who have talked the role of state in pro agricultural policy with the purpose to assure secured livelihood to millions spreaded all over the world.

In the Fifth Henry Simons Lecture delivered at the Law School, University of Chicago, James Tobin (1981 Nobel Laureate in Economics), spoke of "specific egalitarianism," which he defined as "non-market egalitarian distributions of commodities essential to life and citizenship". As Tobin said "In some instances, notably education and medical care, a specific egalitarian distribution today may be essential for improving the distribution of human capital and earning capacity tomorrow" [2]. Rural and Agricultural credit was not merely a commodity that needed to reach the poor to free them from usurious moneylenders; it could also be seen as a *public good* critical to the development of a backward agrarian economy like India.[3]

Raj felt "there are important reasons why banking enterprises seeking to maximise their profits would not venture out into areas and sectors of activity to which high priority needs to be attached from a larger social and economic point of view" (Raj, 1974, p.308)[4]. Private Banks operating in an imperfect credit market would only aggravate already existing imperfections. Keynes and Kalecki had already provided the theoretical foundations of this view in the 1930s. As Kalecki put it, "the most important prerequisite for becoming an entrepreneur is the ownership of capital . . . firms below a certain size has no access whatever to the capital market . . . a state of business democracy where anybody endowed with entrepreneurial ability can obtain capital for starting a business venture is, to put it mildly, unrealistic"[5].

[1]Dow, Sheila C (1985), "*Macroeconomic Thought: A Methodological Approach*". Oxford: Blackwell.

[2]Tobin, J. (1970), "On Limiting the Domain of Inequality", *Journal of Law and Economics*, 13, (2), Pp. 276-277.

[3]Shah Mihir,Rao Rangu and Vijay Shankar P.S. (2007), " Rural Credit in 20th Century India: Overview of History and Perspectives", *Economic and Political Weekly*, 42, 15, Pp. 14–20.

[4]Raj K N (1974), "Monetary Management and Nationalization of Banking in India" in A. Mitra (ed) *Economic Theory and Planning: Essays In Honour of A K Dasgupta*, Oxford University Press.

[5]Kalecki, M. (1954), "*Theory of Economic Dynamics*", Pp. 91-95.

In the *General Theory of money and interest*, John Maynard Keynes points out the problem a slight differently. Keynes distinguishes "two types of risk that affects the volume of investment". The borrower's risk arises because she is unsure whether her business venture will provide the expected yield. They would want a low rate of interest, especially if her venture is a risky one. But the same situation creates the "lender's risk" of default by the borrower (voluntary, what Keynes terms "moral hazard" or involuntary, due to poor returns on investment). This necessitates that the lender charges a rate of interest high enough to induce him to lend. Keynes expresses the resulting social dilemma somewhat poetically: "the hope of a very favourable outcome, which may balance the risk in the mind of the borrower, is not available to solace the lender"[1].

Applying the insights of Keynes and Kalecki to a deeply unequal agrarian economy like India, Raj argues "the very basis of profit-making in banking activity sets limits in underdeveloped economies to the enterprise it can display". There are high information and transaction costs of dealing with many small borrowers that acts as a major disincentive. Also because profitability of banks is greater, the higher "the proportion of their earning assets to the idle cash reserves they have to hold", servicing illiterate customers, who insist on payments in cash on the spot, means higher idle cash reserves of banks and lower profitability. Raj showed that mere legislation and control had not led to an "optimal allocation of investible resources". Nationalisation of large banks was the only forward. Raj was aware that "the bureaucratic element in decision making may introduce considerable rigidity" but he hastened to add that in "large private banks the element of impersonality, with all the rigidity it introduces, is almost as great as in the case of State-owned banks, except in case of favoured customers known to the bank. The larger private banks are no less impervious to the needs of small customers who have no security to offer"[2].

Though Amartya Sen's (1998 Nobel Laureate in Economics) contributions were focused on welfare of people and Social Choice, the agriculture, no longer is neglected because of its intertwined relation with the welfare of the people and food security[3]. Sen's thought in agriculture also carried by Prabhat Patnaik (emeritus professor of JNU), in his words "The significant area which occupied Sen was the economics of agriculture. Sen's interest was stimulated by the Farm Management Studies' finding that if family inputs were evaluated at imputed prices then small farms were loss-making".

---

[1]Keynes J.M. (1935), *"The General Theory of Employment, Interest and Money"*, Pp. 144-145.

[2]Raj K N (1974), Op.Cit, Pp. 307-311.

[3]Sen A and Dreze J (1989), *"Hunger and Public Action"*, Oxford.

Sen explained the continued existence of such 'deficit farms' by the fact that their objectives were different, i.e., they were driven by a different rationality from that of capitalist farms, On the basis of this perception he explained the observed inverse relationship between farm size and productivity per acre (1962) and then went on to produce his well-known article on 'Peasants and Dualism' in the *Journal of Political Economy* (1966) which represents the most rigorous formulation of this genre of theorising on the peasant economy, a genre which constitutes an important though particular approach-often referred to as 'neo-populist'[1] to the agrarian question. The above said theoretical point also properly brought to limelight by Mihir shah[2] in the seminal work on rural credit[3] and confirmed that the life of rural Indians are in disaster, especially when thousands of farmers are already being driven to suicide.

Programmes of directed credit attempts to intervene in the way that banks allocate credit. Without government intervention, the bank will not allocate funds to those projects for which the social returns are the highest. This is true even in the absence of technological spillovers. But, these are benefits that conventional banking might simply ignore. By the same way, the widespread problems many banks faced when real estate markets collapsed provide strong evidence that financial institutions failed to take social returns into account in making real estate loans, Directed credit may be desirable.[4]

Ever since the two rounds of nationalisation of major commercial banks in 1969 and 1980, directed credit has continued to be an integral part of monetary policy. As monetary policy in India has the twin objectives of growth and price stability, the growth objective in a way is embodied in the credit targets.[5] From the prevailing Directed Credit scenario, though the narashiman committee has recommended a phasing out of the directed credit programmes the government. This study aims in analysing the determinants relating to supply of agricultural credit at Macro, Meso[6] (Bank) and Micro (Household) level. The above said aim also founded with the argument by Shashanka Bhide[7] in his path breaking work that the significance of

---

[1]Patnaik U (1979), "Neo-Populism and Marxism", *Journal of Peasant Studies, Pp. 54-63.*

[2]He is a renowned development economist and social worker and Currently Member, Planning Commission, GoI.

[3]Shah Mihir, Rao Rangu and Vijay Shankar P.S. (2007), Op.Cit.

[4]Joseph Stiglitz, Jaime Jaramillo Vallejo and Yung Park (1993), "The Role of the State in Financial Markets", *World Bank Research Observer*, Annual Conference on Development Economics Supplement, pp.19- 61.

[5]EPWRF (2011), "A New Orientation to Directed Credit", *Economic and Political Weekly*, 67, 22, pp.100-106.

[6]Between Macro and Micro Level, this word is coined out of anonymous reference.

[7]Shashanka Bide, R. Meeenashi and Vani B.P. (2005), *"Do Macro Economic Conditions Matter for Agriculture? The Indian Experience"*, Working Paper No. 162, ISEC.

macroeconomic conditions to the agricultural sector and observed that the sector is not insulated from macroeconomic shocks.

Basic Frame Work of this Study

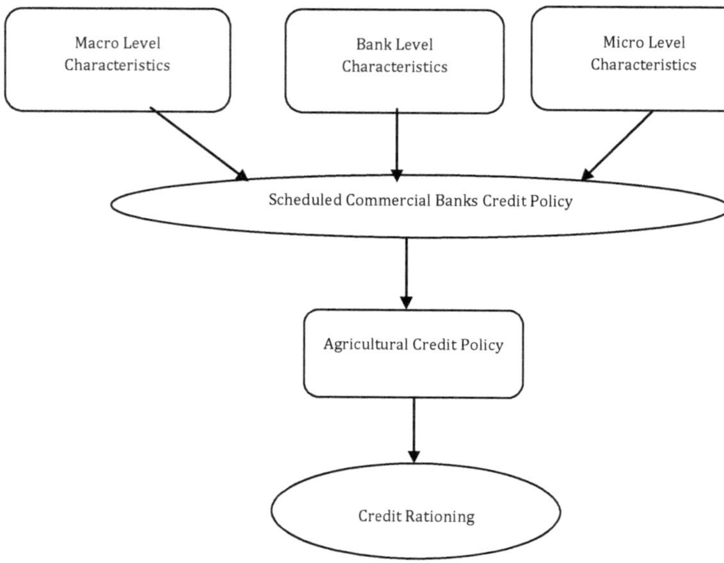

Macro Economic Characteristics and Commercial Bank Credit to Agriculture

The macro level determinants play an important role in driving the flow of institutional credit to priority sector and agriculture as well. The policy on agricultural finance at macro level primarily concerns with the levels of credit flow to agriculture, terms and conditions under which it made available, allocation of credit between sub-sectors (production and investment) to the needy farmers, encouraging them to adopt new agricultural technology and pre and post appraisal of loan disbursement.[1] Macroeconomic models evolve over time due to various externalities. Some of the macroeconomic models of the Indian economy are focusing on output, the fiscal sector and external sector. A survey of the existing macro models indicate that while there is a harmony on certain aspects of the economy, there are other areas that are less than fully understood. Depending on their objective and focus different models have been adopted at different levels of disaggregation at the sector levels. Though there are variations, in general, economic activities have been classified into four sectors, such as agriculture,

[1]Gagan Bihari Sahu (2002), Op. Cit.

manufacturing, service and public administration. Intra-sectoral disaggregation levels have also differed from model to model depending on the objective of the model builder.

Most model builders have disaggregated the agriculture into food grains and non-food grains sector. Ahluwalila and Rangarajan (1986) differentiated between food grains and non-food grains sector. The agriculture sector is the primary supplier of raw materials and food grains for the Indian economy. In most of the models, agriculture sector is taken as supply determined. The total output in this sector is determined by technology, natural resources, land area, water, fertiliser and capital stock. All these variables are expected to affect the production positively. The provision of this input is important because credit or loan-able fund is viewed as more than just another resource such as labour, land, equipment and raw materials (Shepard 1979)[1]. Duong and Izumida (2002)[2] points out that farm credit are not only required by the limitation of self-finance but also uncertainty pertaining to the level of farm inputs and output and the time lag between input and output. There is a need for institutional finance in agriculture development where commercial banks take the lead to fulfill the requirements.

The previous empirical studies on the importance of bank lending or credit channel of monetary policy fall into two broad strategies. The first strategy relies on aggregate data. It usually involves the examination of reaction of bank loans, deposits and bonds to monetary policy shocks, using impulse response functions from a Vector-Auto Regression (VAR) model[3] and reduced-form methods. The impact of macroeconomic variables based on aggregate level of data limited in terms of quantification in supply and demand of credit at different institutional level. The impulse response functions captures the shock in accurate way but is used only as an indicator. A number of studies based on VAR have examined whether the credit channel is operating alongside the interest rate channel by using aggregate data. Many studies have shown that bank loans decline after a monetary policy shock, but these findings are weighed down by the identification problems, as it remains unclear whether the drop is driven by the loan supply or loan demand effects. While the credit channel emphasises a shift in loan supply, the interest rate channel stresses a shift in loan demand, which stems from a policy-induced decline in real activity.[4] Some ground breaking work claimed that distinguishing

[1]Shepard (1979), *"Market Power and Economic Welfare"*, New York Random house.

[2]Duong and Izumida (2002), "Does Regulation Improve Small Farmers", *Journal of Development Economics, 33*(1), Pp. 67-87.

[3]Sims introduced and got Nobel in 2011.

[4]Brooks and Petya Koeva (2007), *"Does the Bank Lending Channel of Monetary Transmission Work in Turkey?"*, European Department, IMF Working Paper No. WP/07/272, December.

between these predictions is a difficult task as it is not possible using reduced-form estimates based on aggregate data alone, to identify whether bank balance sheet contractions are caused by shifts in loan supply or loan demand.

Bank Level Determinants and Commercial Bank Credit to Agriculture

The second strategy uses bank-level data. Such a strategy attempts to identify shifts in loan supply from shifts in loan demand. The presumption is that certain bank characteristics determine the degree to which banks respond to policy shocks. Most studies specify loan growth for each bank as a function of its lagged values, aggregate variables (GDP growth, short-term interest rate change, and inflation) and bank-specific characteristics (size, liquidity and capitalisation). However, this strategy does not address the issue that the change in monetary policy may not be exogenous which makes it hard to identify the true effect of higher interest rates on loan supply.[1]

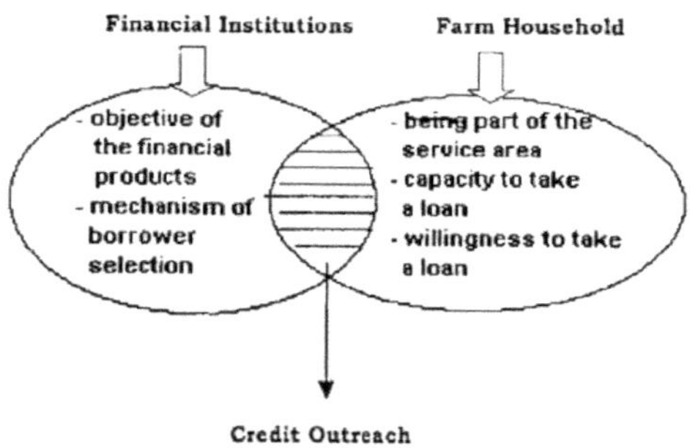

Gagan Bihari Sahu Model (2002)

Several articles focused on the need for banking sector to improve their lending schemes. The existing bank level data shows that banks are not sufficiently supporting the Priority sector lending, which in turn is going to have big impact on the agricultural sector itself. The factors like branch operations, number of branches in rural areas, financial inclusion and its impact, credit deposit ratio, lending policies, RBI policy, sectoral development and other factors are analysed with empirical evidence and statistical relevance.[2] This study tries to do an empirical research to show how Bank level factor works at micro level.

---

[1]Huelsewig, Oliver, Eric Mayer and Timo Wollmershaeuser (2005), "*Bank loan supply and monetary policy transmission in Germany: an assessment based on matching impulse responses*," CESIFO Working Paper No. 1380, January.

[2]Subramaniam and Ravi Subramaniam (2009), Op. Cit, *http://ssrn.com/abstract=1483243.*

Micro Level Determinants and Agriculture Credit by Commercial Banks

Institutional Credit performs a noteworthy function in supporting modern production technologies and private investments on the farms by facilitating sufficient amount for the agriculture sector of India even for many developing countries where the majority population depends on agriculture, flow of funds is cyclical and income and savings of the farmers are low. However, it also acts like a double-edged weapon; if it is used productively it raises productivity and production, but if it is used irrationally on unproductive activities, it leads to the problem of indebtedness. Several studies have shown that institutional credit has contributed positively to the adoption of modern production inputs and private investments in tube well irrigation, tractorisation and other farm machinery, which has contributed towards the growth of the agriculture sector[1].

Institutional credit is supplied in the form of production credit where as investment credit is supplied to farming sector for incurring expenditure on, variable production inputs like fertilisers, seeds, agro-chemicals, labour hiring, machinery hiring, fuel and oil, electric motor charges, etc., private capital formation such as irrigation facility, tractors and other machinery, land development, etc. Equity issues involved in institutional agricultural credit are widely debated across India. Various farm level studies have shown that the access to institutional finance of smallholders is limited and inadequate. The main intention of this part is to study about dissimilarity in the access to credit and what makes some farm households to reach formal credit and others not. This part also touches on what basis, bankers determine the credit limit to the borrower. The following earlier studies have been conducted by various researchers in the above themes that have been discussed so far. A review of these studies enabled the researcher to formulate the present study. Further, the reviews of previous studies have divided according to the conceived framework of the study.

Previous Studies on Scheduled Commercial Banks Policy and Issues in Credit

Subramaniam and Ravi Subramaniam[2] (2009) stressed on the Indian banking sectors' commitment to level down the agricultural sector in lending. They point out that India's rising population requires more food production to meet its own demand. This work noted that the agricultural sector has pushed as secondary sector rather than primary. This article focuses on the need for banking sector to consider improving their lending schemes. The primary objective of the author is to highlight that banks data are not sufficiently supporting the

---

[1]Sidhu, Kamal Vatta and Arjinder Kaur (2008), "Dynamics of Institutional Agricultural Credit and Growth in Punjab: Contribution and Demand-Supply Gap, *Agricultural Economics Research Review*, Vol. 21, Pp. 407-414.

[2]Subramaniam and Ravi Subramaniam (2009), Op. Cit, *http://ssrn.com/abstract=1483243.*

Priority sector lending, which in turn is going to have big impact on the agricultural sector itself. The factors like branch operations, number of branches in rural areas, financial inclusion and its impact, credit deposit ratio, lending policies, RBI policy, sectoral development and other factors are analysed with empirical evidence and statistical relevance. Authors suggest that agricultural sector wants more consideration from union government and also they should observe how their policies are implemented in banks. Authors asked the researchers to drive their academic and empirical research to show how rural branches at micro level functions. This study gives an opinion that the RBIs need to revise their standards to understand that still India is agriculture based economy and a developing country like India needs to grow, first rural poverty need to be eradicated.

Ramakumar[1] (2009) observed that agricultural development in post-independence India is marked by a historic failure of the state to resolve the agrarian question, i.e., ending the extreme concentration of land ownership and use and weakening of the factors that fostered disincentives in investment and technology adoption, tied workers to a social system with considerable pre-modern features and compressed purchasing power. While this failure has shaped the pattern and nature of agricultural growth in India after 1947, the implementation of economic "reforms" after 1991 has introduced new dimensions to the contradictions of the earlier regime. In the 1990s and 2000s, some of the fundamental contradictions of the post-independence agrarian economy have persisted; on the other hand, some of the pillars on which the earlier regime rested have been undermined. About 40 percentage of the total lending was to be necessarily lent to the priority sectors, which primarily included agriculture. About 10 percentage of the total lending was to be directed to "weaker sections" that included small and marginal cultivators and agricultural labourers. The policy of social and development banking was a supply-led policy; it aimed at augmenting the supply of credit to rural areas, and that too at an affordable interest rate.

Siudek Tomasz[2] (2008) points out that Agricultural credit are to perform many significant purposes and are assumed to play an important role in the development of agriculture. Its main tasks include intensification of farm production, enhancing the agricultural productivity and helping agricultural sector to achieve faster technological, biological and social progress. In Poland, farmers rely primarily on cooperative banks for agricultural credit. This paper is an

[1]Ramakumar R. and Chavan, Pallavi (2007), "Revival of Agricultural Credit in the 2000s: An Explanation", *Economic and Political Weekly*, 42, 52, Pp. 57-63.

[2]Siudek Tomasz (2008), "*Do Farm Credits Stimulate Development of Agriculture in Poland?*", 12th Congress of the European Association of Agricultural Economists–EAAE 2008.

attempt to examine the impact of agricultural credits disbursed by the cooperative banks on regional development of agricultural sector in Poland over 1997-2006. Sources of data include financial statements of the banks (1373 observations) providing credit-related information and sectoral background data for agriculture from Central Statistical Office of Poland. The levels of agricultural development were assessed by using a national-level and regional-level composite indicators constructed by the author by the use of factor analysis. Additionally, one-factor ANOVA, Pearson correlations and linear regression were applied.

Harangus and Daniela[1](2008) gave note of this paper are showed the principal elements for analysis taken into consideration in the crediting process of agriculture. An excessive rigour in the analysis of these elements leads to a limitation of access to banking credits for agricultural farms. The method of this research is based on quantification of flexibility degree of banks granting credits to agricultural customers and finding new solutions in the crediting process of agriculture. It results that the totality of risk factors specific to any activity, including the agricultural farm, can be quantified. Starting with the analysis of risk factors and symptoms, this paper proposes new solutions for diminishing the degree of banks' risks. This study is based on information regarding present circumstances of crediting system for agriculture and regarding the sum of agricultural credits in the total volume of credits granted by banks. The need for credits in agriculture is greater than in other sectors of economy because of the following reasons: Biological laws governing production process in agriculture generate a much slower regeneration of funds and capital, unlike other areas of production, the need for credits being thus much higher; immobilisation of funds in agriculture is higher than the other sectors and the capital of the farmers' is not sufficient; land is expensive but necessary and it represents the main means for production.

Reddy[2] (2008) has talked on Agriculture–emerging issues and possible approaches. RBI's major objectives are to maintain price stability and maintain growth momentum, especially employment generation. In this endeavour, agriculture plays a critical role since agricultural commodities have a relatively significant weight in price indices in our country and also in anchoring inflation expectations. In terms of employment also agriculture dominates, accounting for about sixty percentage of the total, while in terms of GDP its share is less than a one third of that. However, the policy space available to RBI is basically confined to managing

[1]Harangus and Daniela (2008), "New solutions in the crediting process of agriculture http://mpra.ub.uni-muenchen.de/16540/.

[2]Reddy (2008), "*Agriculture–emerging issues and possible approaches*", 40th Convocation Address of the Acharya N G Ranga Agricultural University, Hyderabad, 5 June 2008.

aggregate demand through appropriate stance in regard to growth in money supply, interest and exchange rates and, to some extent, flow of credit through banks. Yet, in view of the criticality of agriculture, RBI articulates its approaches to agriculture through the Annual Reports. This study summarises briefly that the analysis and the views as expressed by the Directors of the RBI in their Annual Reports during the recent past–say for the last five years. Since the mid-1990s, the growth of the agricultural sector has not only been low, but also volatile. The crop yields have shown an unstable trend in recent years. An area of growing concern has been the continued incidence of localised droughts even in good monsoon years. In recent years, the food consumption basket is getting diversified towards value added food products such as meat, poultry, fish, vegetables and fruits. It is important for production to respond to these shifts in consumption.

Satyasai[1] (2008) points out that in the post-economic reforms era, Indian agriculture has been subjected to various external and domestic forces that have compelled the farmers to change their product-mix as well as organization of the farming. Distress has set in the rural economy in many areas, even forcing farmers to commit suicides as an extreme reaction. The major changes that have directly impacted the agricultural sector are financial sector reforms, decontrolling of fertiliser prices, freeing of imports of agricultural commodities, etc. Of these, the financial sector reforms have been crucial in view of its influence on rural credit delivery. The rural credit plays a very crucial role in agriculture and rural economy. And, any disturbance in its delivery mechanism can cause cascading effects. Demand for credit emanates from demand for inputs and services needed for various farm operations. It constitutes a major portion of liquidity with farmers and imparts the much needed purchasing power to the capital-starved farmers. Public policy in the country has always been directed towards ensuring adequate and cheaper credit and adopts institutionalisation of credit as the primary focus.

Ramachandran and Madhura Swaminathan[2](2007) pointed out that financial liberalisation after 1991, decimate the formal system of institutional credit in rural India. It represented a clear and explicit reversal of the policy of social and development banking, such as it was, and contributed in no small way to the extreme deprivation and distress of which the rural poor in India have been victims over the last decade. This paper examines the impact of

---

[1]Satyasai(2008), "Rural Credit Delivery in India: Structural Constraints and Some Corrective Measures, *Agricultural Economics Research Review*, Vol. 21, 2008, Pp. 387-394.

[2]Ramachandran and Madhura Swaminathan (2007)," *Financial Liberalisation and Rural Banking in India,* Paper to be presented at the International Conference organised by the International Development Economics Associates (IDEAs).

changes in banking policy and structure on the rural economy, and on the rural poor in particular. financial liberalisation is a crucial component of the programmes of economic reforms that are being imposed on the people of less-developed countries. Firstly, the supply of formal sector credit to the countryside as a whole has been inadequate. Secondly, rural credit markets in India themselves have been very imperfect and fragmented. Thirdly, as the foregoing suggests, the distribution of formal sector credit has been unequal, particularly with respect to region and class, caste and gender in the countryside. Formal sector credit needs specially to reach backward areas, income-poor households, people of the oppressed castes and tribes, and women. Fourthly, the major source of credit to rural households, particularly income-poor working households, has been the informal sector. Informal sector loans typically are advanced at very high rates of interest. Further, the terms and conditions attached to these loans have given rise to an elaborate structure of coercion–economic and extra-economic burden–in the countryside.

Ramesh Golait[1] (2007) tries to study the issues in agricultural credit in India. This paper reveals that the credit delivery to the agriculture sector continues to be inadequate. The study came to know that the banking system is still hesitant on various grounds to purvey credit to small and marginal farmers. This study points out that the demand for agricultural credit arises due to:

Lack of simultaneity between the realisation of income and act of expenditure;

Lumpiness of investment in fixed capital formation; and

Stochastic surges in capital needs and saving that accompany technological innovations.

This study finds that the flow of investment credit to agriculture is constrained by host of factors such as high transaction costs, structural deficiencies in the rural credit delivery system issues relating to credit worthiness, lack of collaterals in view of low asset base of farmers, low volume of loans with associated higher risks, high man power requirements, *etc.* The large proportion of population in the lower strata, which is having major share in the land holdings, receives much less credit than its requirements. The growing disparity between marginal, small and large farmers continues to be a cause for concern. This observed phenomenon may be attributed to the "risk aversion" attitude of the bankers towards small and marginal farmers as against the large farmers, who are better placed in offering collaterals. The situation calls for concerted efforts to augment the flow of credit to agriculture, alongside exploring new

[1]Ramesh Golait (2007), "Current Issues in Agriculture Credit in India: An Assessment", *Reserve Bank of India Occasional Papers,* 28, 1, summer 2007.

innovations in product design and methods of delivery, through better use of technology and related processes.

Pallavi Chavan[1] (2005) written in response to Priya Basu's article entitled 'A Financial System for India's Poor on September 10, 2005) under the H T Parekh Finance Forum. This article stresses the importance of finance in helping the poor and the underprivileged sections of the population achieving higher economic growth. It discusses the various initiatives taken since independence to develop a financial system that would cater to the needs of rural India, and particularly of agriculture. These initiatives included, first, the establishment of a cooperative credit network in the Indian countryside. This was followed by the nationalisation of commercial banks and directing the flow of credit from these institutions (which essentially had an urban base) to rural areas, and to agriculture. The author refers to this period as the period of social banking. She argues that social banking did not deliver what it had set out to deliver, that is, an *inclusive* financial system. While there was improved access to finance for certain sections of the rural population over the years of social banking, it still left out of its ambit a large section of the rural population, particularly the poor. The author then discusses the period of financial liberalisation that began in the early 1990s, and points out that there is still a hangover of the regulatory measures that were put on the operations of rural financial institutions during the earlier period of social banking. According to the author, the belief underlying the social banking policy was that the "poor are not bankable", and that, banks would cater to these sections only if they were "mandated to do so". The author feels that this belief continues to influence the Indian rural banking policy. Hence, she argues for a more liberalised and competitive rural financial systems, in which banks are given greater operational freedom than at present. Her suggested reform measures include making priority sector lending obligations "tradable", which would provide better incentives to banks to deal with rural borrowers.

Previous Studies on Macroeconomic Characteristics and Credit Policy

Ramachandran and Rawal[2] (2010) describe and analyse the impact of policies of globalisation and liberalisation on the agrarian economy of India. In particular, it discusses the reversal of land reform, changes in the policies of administered agricultural input costs and output prices, cutbacks in public investment in rural, physical and social infrastructure, the

[1]Pallavi Chavan (2005), "How 'Inclusive' Are Banks under Financial Liberalisation?", *Economic and Political Weekly,* October 22, 2005.

[2]Ramachandran, V.K. and Rawal, Vikas (2010) "The Impact of Liberalization and Globalization on India's Agrarian Economy," *Global Labour Journal*: 1, 1, Pp. 56-91.

dismantling of the institutional structure of social and development banking, the withdrawal of quantitative restrictions on the import of agricultural products, cutbacks in the public distribution system, and the undermining of national systems of research and extension and protection of national plant and other biological wealth. The data used in the paper come from the major sources of national-level official statistics and primary data collected as part of a Project on Agrarian Relations in India. This paper begins with a discussion of land reform and landlordism. They discussed the interconnections between landlordism, moneylender-merchant exploitation and caste and gender oppression in the countryside, and argue that neo-liberalism has not lessened the tactical or strategic importance of addressing these issues. They concluded that there are three features of the current situation that we shall highlight. The major force on the left in India considers the Indian state to be the organ of the class rule of the bourgeoisie and landlords, led by the big bourgeoisie, who are in increasing collaboration–as a junior partner or subordinate ally–of imperialism. This is the view of the state that informs this paper, and the researchers' cannot emphasise enough that nothing in the present situation has undone landlordism as a fundamental barrier to agrarian and general social progress.

Chadrasekar[1] (2009) quoted that there are three immediate effects that the financial crisis had for the real economy. First, it resulted in a collapse of the credit-financed consumption and investment boom since collapsing housing and stock values' sharply curtailed demand. The collapse in demand was aggravated by the unwillingness of financial institutions which are overloaded with defaulting borrowers and worthless assets to lend. And finally, all of this was worsened by the insolvency of financial firms including the banks, which even threatened the payments and settlements system. The agricultural sector, exposed by liberalisation to global trends, is bound to be affected diversely by the collapse in commodity prices associated with the global recession. With its viability under challenge because of long years of neglect during the era of liberalisation and the finance-led boom in the Indian economy, this fall in prices is bound to severely damage the earnings and livelihood of the large mass of the peasantry and the agricultural labourers.

Somoye and Bamidele[2] (2009) pointed out that there are fundamental economic roles banks are expected to perform, especially that of acting as financial intermediaries and

[1]Chadrasekar C.P. (2009), "Global Economic Crisis And Its Impact On The Agrarian Situation In India", *Financial Liberalisation and Rural Credit in India.*

[2]Somoye, Russell Olukayode Christopher and Ilo, Bamidele M (2009), " Economic Risks of Banks", Journal of Money, Investment and Banking, 288, Pp. 88-100.

facilitating the payment system for the purpose of ensuring an efficient allocation of the deposits in their custody. Banks typically make out loans in order to generate income and make the bulk of their income from the spread between lending and deposit rates relative to the volume of loans granted. The volume of loans granted by a bank in a year may be a function of its internal characteristics such as size, deposit base, liquidity, credit policy and other internal factors, all of which may be said to fall though relatively, within the control of the bank. The study therefore, recommends that while banks should pay adequate attention to the consequences of their firm specific characteristics in their lending activities both in the short-run and long-run, their worries about macroeconomic instability should be limited to the long-run consequences on their lending behaviour. It is also pertinent that appropriate measures to be taken to curtail inflation and sporadic money supply, growth making banks become unfavourably disposed to lending given the attendant negative consequences of loan curtailment on economic growth in the long run.

Sidhu et al.,[1] (2008) told that the demand for capital increases with transformation of the agriculture sector from traditionalism towards commercialisation. The seed of commercialisation in Punjab agriculture was sown with the introduction of high-yielding varieties of wheat and rice, followed by use of chemical fertilisers and investments in irrigation, especially on tubewells, agro-chemicals to control weeds, diseases and insect-pests management, and tractorisation to ensure timeliness and precision in farm operations. The data on disbursement of credit over time were taken from the published documents of Reserve Bank of India, while the data on use of intermediate production inputs were collected from a randomly selected sample of 160 farmers, representing all the three agro-climatic zones and all farm-size groups in the state. The data included variable inputs for all crops, such as seed, fertilisers and manures, pesticides, hired labourers, hired machinery, diesel and mobile oil use, marketing expenses, minor repairs, etc. During the period 1985 to 1995, the growth of institutional agricultural credit has been found to slow down, whereas demand for capital had increased in the wake of degradation of natural resources like soil and groundwater and deceleration of output growth. Consequently, the role of non-institutional sources in financing capital requirements was increased and led to the problem of indebtedness due to unscrupulous nature of such loans along with decelerating growth.

---

[1]R.S. Sidhu, Kamal Vatta and Arjinder Kaur (2008), "Dynamics of Institutional Agricultural Credit and Growth in Punjab: Contribution and dmand-Supply Gap, Agricultural Economics Research Review, Vol. 21, Pp. 407-414.

Khan et.al. [1] **(2007)** has examined (i) the nature and extent of inter-state disparities in per hectare flow of short-term institutional credit to agriculture, and (ii) its relationship with average cost of cultivation across states. This paper has covered all the six regions of the country comprising seventeen agriculturally most important states having about 96 percentage agricultural land in the country. This study has found that inter-regional disparities in per hectare flow of institutional credit as measured through coefficient of variation (CV) had increased during the pre-liberalisation period between 1980-81 and 1990-91. During the post-liberalisation era (1991-92 to 2001- 02), the inter-regional disparities have reduced. The per hectare institutional credit flow has shown that in most of the states across the country, the coverage has increased though in different degrees during the post liberalisation stage over the pre-liberalisation period. In this connection, the financial institutions need to intensify their focus on agriculture and should regularly update the crop-wise scale of finance in line with the rising cost of cultivation. The renewed policy thrust given to the institutional agricultural credit in the union budgets of 2005-06 and 2006-07 is expected to be helpful in this context.

Sahu[2] **(2007)** studied about the factors influencing variation in agricultural credit flow to various states of India. He points out that the regions in Indian are economically relatively backward having less access to institutional credit than other areas. This study justified that there is dearth of empirical studies dealing with causes of variation in the quantum of agricultural credit across the states in India is the reason lying to undertake the study. The author examined the extent of interstate variations in the supply of institutional credit for agriculture by using data since 1981-2000. This seeks to study the supply of credit flow to 14 major states in India namely, Andhra Pradesh, Bihar, Gujarat, Haryana, Maharashtra, Orissa, Punjab, Rajasthan, Tamil Nadu, Uttar Pradesh, Madhya Pradesh, Karnataka, Kerala and West Bengal. This paper also disclosed that the growth rate of agricultural credit which was uneven during sub periods as well as across the states. The analysis found that there are interstate differences in the access to credit as well as the loan amount obtained by farmers' households even for the same size class of land holding. This paper concludes that for better provisioning of agricultural credit, the increasing of credit to deposit ratio should be backed by more irrigation facility and banking infrastructure.

---

[1]Khan A.R., S.K. Tewari and Shukla A.N. (2007), "Effect of Liberalization on Institutional Agricultural Credit Flow and its Relationship with Average Cost of Cultivation in Indian Agriculture", *Agricultural Economics Research Review*, 20, Pp. 227-23.

[2]Gagan Bihari Sahu (2007), "Supply Analysis of Institutional Credit to Agriculture for Major States in India", *Indian Journal of Agricultural Economics*, 62, 4, Pp. 664-678.

Previous Studies on Bank Characteristics and Credit Policy

Mahendra Dev[1] (2009) provided an overview of the issues and policies on the impact of structural macro policy reforms on agriculture and reforms relating to supply side factors in agriculture sectors. This study concludes that the structural reforms on agriculture have positive and negative effects and the slowing in agriculture growth could be attributed to the structural factors on the supply side such as public investment, credit, technology, land and water management etc. rather than globalisation and trade reforms. There are six deficits in Indian agriculture. These are: (a) investment, credit and Infrastructure deficit; (b) land and water management deficit; (c) research and extension (technology) deficit; (d) market deficit; (e) diversification deficit; (f) institutions deficit. Reforms are needed to reduce these deficits in order to achieve the following goals of agriculture: (i) Achieving 4% growth in agriculture; (ii) equity in terms of higher growth in lagging regions, small and marginal farmers and women and; (iii) sustainability. Apart from high growth, efficiency (cost reduction) is also needed in globalised world. There is a need to concentrate on delivery systems also. India's large numbers of farmers can benefit if there are right policies and effective implementation.

Satish and Nirupam[2] (2009) told that Indian agriculture is structurally small farm and smallholder based. The 1990s also witnessed the rise of microfinance as an alternative to the weakened rural credit markets. In India, the Self Help Group(SHG)-Bank linkage programme linking banking sector credit to informal groups grew manifold to emerge as the largest microfinance programme in the world. However, existing forms of microfinance and microenterprise financing might be unsuitable to fully serve the credit needs of agriculture. Additionally, tenant farmers and oral lessees without land to serve as collateral, find it difficult to access credit from mainstream banks. In order to address this, innovations in microfinance technologies like the Joint Liability Group, the Kerala model of horticulture development which identify collateral substitutes present interesting alternatives. This discussion showed that the contribution of small farms to agricultural growth and India's food security is unmatched by any other class of farms. Despite this, small farms have not received the support of institutional mechanisms especially credit supply since the financial sector reforms began in the 1990s. Microfinance seen as the solution for all credit deprived sections of the economy also has been unable to meet the requirements of agriculture because of its inherent weaknesses. Public policy in countries like India should emphasise on strengthening and expanding the

---

[1]Mahendra Dev (2009), "Challenges for Revival of Indian Agriculture", *Agricultural Economics Research Review*, 22, Pp. 21-45.

[2]Satish and Nirupam (2009), *"Credit Markets for Small Farms: Role for Institutional Innovations"*, 111 EAAE-IAAE Seminar 'Small Farms: decline or persistence' University of Kent, Canterbury, UK.

institutional credit delivery mechanisms for agriculture. This involves revitalising and expanding the cooperative credit structure and the rural banking network and the adoption of policies to ensure the flow of credit to agriculture.

Janda[1] (2009) pointed out that the government supported finances have a very vital part in the financing of the agriculture in transition economies. Upto the end of the 80's, the government's support of agriculture in all transition economies had a very different nature and forms as compared to the situation in the 90's. In the pre-reform period, agriculture in all transition countries was administratively isolated from the world market, so the export and import interventions had very different forms from those used in market economies. This paper provides an econometric estimation of the influence of individual social-economic, natural, and technological determinants of the credit provision for the agriculture in the case of the Czech Republic. The regression model is based on the microeconomic model of the maximization of the bank's profit. The results of this paper show that the support of agricultural credit provided by Guarantee Fund goes primarily to the areas with good conditions for the development of agricultural production. On the other hand, the direct government subsidies are targeted primarily to the areas with non-favourable natural conditions. The influence of the factors determining the provision of the agricultural credit in the Czech Republic is analysed on the cross-section of the county data. Out of 76 Czech counties, this work has used 63 counties in my analyses. The removed 13 counties correspond to large town agglomerations and to the counties with missing or unreliable data. As a dependent variable in my regressions, use the volume of credit supported by Guarantee Fund per hectare of agricultural land in a given county. The data on supported credit for 1996 include only the period from the beginning of the year up to the September 10, 1996. Besides the three regression equations with the supported credit in the years 1994–6 as a dependent variable, also estimate two equations with the value of direct subsidies per hectare in 1994–95 as a dependent variable.

Deepak Shah[2] (2007) says that Credit flows through the cooperatives in rural India and their sustainability, viability and operational efficiency have become the major focus of attention of various policymakers in the era of financial sector reforms. Although reforms in the banking sector were initiated in commercial banks much earlier (beginning 1991-92), the

[1]Janda, Karel (2009), *"The Roles of Commercial Credit and Direct Subsidies in Czech Agriculture during Early Transition"*, http://mpra.ub.uni-muenchen.de/17005/.

[2]Deepak Shah (2007), "Banking Sector Reforms and Co-operative Credit Institutions in Maharashtra: A Synthesis", *Agricultural Economics Research Review*, 20, Pp. 235-254.

reform process in the cooperatives has taken a longer time to get started. It was because of the need for generating a consensus among various state governments which govern and control the cooperative credit institutions and to balance the interests of many diversified groups. The credit cooperatives in Maharashtra have shown slower growth in their membership and institutional financing. On the other hand, a faster growth has been observed in outstandings against loan advances. A decline in the loan advances with rise in GCA in the Konkan region is another issue, but the most important one among all is the mounting overdues and non-performing assets (NPAs) of the cooperatives operating in both forward and backward regions of Maharashtra. The viability of two central level credit institutions, viz. Sangli District Central Cooperative Bank and Buldana District Central Cooperative Bank, has been estimated. In order to rejuvenate the rural credit delivery system through cooperatives, the major problems facing the system, viz. high transaction cost, poor repayment performance, mounting NPAs, distributional aspect of credit, low coverage of SC/ST members, etc. need to be tackled with more fiscal jurisprudence reserving exemplary punishment for willful defaults, particularly by the large farmers.

Nachane et. al.[1] (2006) noted that the banking structure that India inherited at Independence in 1947 suffered from two major drawbacks: (i) interlocking of directorship of industry houses and banks, and (ii) paucity of credit to socially and economically important sectors of the economy. The numerous problems arising in the wake of these drawbacks provided the economic rationale for the momentous decision to nationalize 14 private banks in 1969, as well as for the subsequent nationalization of six more banks in 1980. The post-nationalization phase was characterized by a strategy of massive expansion of the banking network coupled with stipulations on sectoral lending. Even today, when the euphoria over nationalization has given way to considerable skepticism, it cannot be denied that the liberal branch licensing norms coupled with a system of directed credit stipulations, made a significant dent on rural and (to some extent) urban poverty and mitigated the dependence of the socially and economically disadvantaged groups on the indigenous money lenders. Additionally many would agree that the system did contribute to rapid growth by providing timely and concessional credit to several industrial sectors. In the financial sector specifically, the thrust of the reforms was to promote a diversified, efficient and competitive financial system. While these reforms were underway, the world economy also witnessed significant changes, coinciding with the movement towards global integration of financial services.

---

[1]Nachane, Saibal Ghosh and Partha Ray (2006), *"Banking in India"*, http://mpra.ub.uni-muenchen.de/17539/.

Alina Danilowska[1] **(2005)** pointed out that, in May 2004 Poland joined the European Union. It means involving in Common Agricultural Policy. The accession will result the end of agricultural preferential credit system, which has existed since 1994. It seems that the evaluation of outcomes of the system is necessary. It can help to understand dimensions of credit as a tool of intervention and to recognize constrains, advantages and disadvantages of it using. The analysis of results of credit interventionism starts with characteristics of the Polish agriculture and its role in the economy at the beginning of the transition. It is followed by the description of the first steps of credit intervention in agriculture. The next part is devoted to presentation of basic assumptions, formal aims, and elements of the credit preferential system. In the third part, the result of the 10 years it's functioning is examined. To sum up the comparison losses and gains is given. The examined period covers generally 10 years from 1994 to 2003. he analysis showed that during 10 years of the running the system about 10% of farms were its beneficiaries. The positive changes in agricultural sector took place but it is difficult to separate the credit assistance effects. The system has the advantageous influence on the creation of the sustainable financial system in the rural areas by helping cooperatives banks to overcome difficulties by generating stable farmers' credit demand.

Bard et. al. [2] **(2000)** investigate about the effects of commercial bank structure and other characteristics on agriculture lending and a case loan request methodology is adopted to evaluate how changes in commercial banking structure are influencing credit availability and terms for selected farm business types. This study utilizes a different approach for data generation to evaluate the effects of changes in the banking industry on agricultural credit delivery. They assess the differences in credit terms among three borrower types by evaluating lenders responses to the case loan requests. This paper make an enquiry on the loan decision process determines how much to lend to the prospective borrower as well as other credit terms. To determine how the bank characteristics influence the loan amount and interest rate TOBIT and OLS estimations are employed and paired comparisons approach is used to evaluate the differences in credit terms among the borrower types. This paper finds that lenders tend to exert their financial control more over capital financing requests than over operating loans. They noted that the major thrust of this study was to access the effects of bank

---

[1]Alina Danilowska (2005), "The Credit Support System in the Polish Agriculture. The Evaluation of 10 Years Performances", *Paper prepared for presentation at the 99th seminar of the EAAE (European Association of Agricultural Economists), 'title', place, country, date as in: August 24-27.*

[2]Bard, Peter, and Paul (2000), "Effects of Commercial Bank Structure and Other Characteristics on Agriculture Lending", *Agricultural Finance Review,* 60, Pp. 17-31.

characteristics on the cost and availability of agricultural credit. Through the primary data, they found that some bank characteristics significantly influenced the credit terms, they did not influence the credit terms in an economically significant manner or in a systematic pattern. They concluded that a few bank characteristics were found to influence loan interest rates, Bank amount did not appear to affect loan amounts significantly.

Eustacius et.al. [1] **(1995)** examines the factors affecting commercial bank lending to agriculture in United States of America. They pointed out that the commercial banks have traditionally played an important role in financing agriculture, their commitment fluctuates. TOBIT econometric procedure was used in this study to examine the effects of selected demand and supply factors on agriculture lending. They examine the impact of increased commercial bank reliance on the interest sensitive deposits after de regulation which allows banks to allot towards agriculture relative to other investment opportunities. This study took the data from FIDC call reports on condition and income, agriculture data are collected from the census of agriculture. This empirical paper shows that the commercial banks deposit become more sensitive to market rates, the proportion of agricultural loans relative to commercial bank assets decline. This work also reveals that bank affiliated with multi bank holding companies lend less money to agriculture relative to their assets than non-multi bank holding company affiliates and there is an absolute reduction in the total amount of loans available to the agriculture sector. This study concluded that recent de regulation of commercial banks has affected the agriculture lending adversely.

Previous Studies on Household Characteristics and Credit Policy

Rahji and Adeoti[2] **(2010)** identified the determinants affecting commercial banks decision to ration agricultural credit in south western-Nigeria. They pointed out that farm credit has long been identified as a major input in the development of agricultural sector in Nigeria. They found that the decline the contribution of the sector to the Nigerian economy has been attributed to the lack of a formal institutional credit Policy and paucity of credit institutions can assist farmers among other things. Data were sourced from the rural branches of four principal commercial banks in Ibadan. They have released the data on anonymous basis. This study employs logit model to predict the results. This study recommended that the farm land redistribution, farm income improvement, gender specific and credit allocation policies to the

[1]Eustacius and Leatham, (1995), "Factors Affecting Commercial Bank Lending to Agriculture", *J.Agr. and Applied Econ.*, 27 (1) , July, Pp. 112-126.

[2]Rahji and Adeoti (2010), "Determinants of Agricultural Credit Rationing by Commercial Banks in South-Western, Nigeria", *International Journal of Finance and Economics*, 37, Pp. 7-14.

crop sub-sector were recommended. The results of the study tend to support a preference for cash crops against food crops by the lending institutions. There is the need for food crop farmers to benefit from agricultural loans by the banks as well.

Mahadeva Murthy et.al.[1] (2009) points out that Agriculture is a way of life, a tradition, which for centuries, has shaped the thought, the outlook, the culture and the economic life of the people of India. Nearly 61 percentage of the workforce depends upon agriculture for livelihood. Credit is a vital factor of the production function, more so in Indian agriculture. The present paper aims at studying the institutional finance for agricultural activities, loan outstanding by institutional finance, correlation co-efficient between institutional credit and loan outstanding by credit agencies. Since the multi-agency approach to agricultural credit was accepted, four agencies, consisting of (1) Government; (2) Co-operatives; (3) Commercial Banks; and (4) Regional Rural Banks were financing. The paper concludes that institutional credit has played a vital role in supporting cultural production in India and the amount of institutional credit for agriculture and allied activities has increased over the years.

Mustapha Jouili[2] (2009) utter that, In Tunisia, small and medium-sized family farms dominate agriculture. From the early 80s, with the introduction of the Structural Adjustment Program (SAP), the conditions of production and reproduction of small farms have radically changed. In addition to the unfavorable trend of the prices, these farms are increasingly excluded from credit, land and support services. Small farms are also hampered by increasingly restricted access to different resources. New forms of regulation of agricultural activity have actually resulted in a modification of terms of access to finance, land and various support services, with marginalization of small and medium-sized farms. The submission of financing agriculture to rules of profitability has resulted in limited and increasingly differentiated access of farms to sources of institutional funding. An analysis in terms of numbers of farms integrated in the system of institutional funding, shows that the scope of agricultural credit remains obviously limited. The large farms have no difficulty to borrow. Those who seek to maintain their plots are in the extreme insecurity. Thus, without necessarily causing their real and effective disappearance globalization ruins small farms.

[1]Mahadeva Murthy, Suresh and Veena (2009), "Dimensions of Institutional Finance for Agricultural Activities : An Analysis", *Indian Management Studies Journal*,13, Pp. 13-30.

[2]Mustapha Jouili (2009), *"Tunisian agriculture: Are small farms doomed to disappear?"*, 111 EAAE-IAAE Seminar 'Small Farms: decline or persistence' University of Kent, Canterbury, UK.

Akram et. al[1] **(2008)** examine about the agricultural credit constraints and borrowing behavior of farmers in rural Punjab. They pointed out that the farmers were facing many constraints to avail agricultural credit in a timely fashion and they noted that the collateral was one of the major constraints. Two data sets were utilized for the paper. The data from Pakistan rural house hold survey and farm survey of 160 farm house holds was conducted in the summer 2007 from the Sargodha region, Punjab. This work estimated the borrowing behavior of the respondents through LOGIT model and identified the determinants of credit constraints. The findings reveal that the transitory income, educational level and predicted interest rate have important bearing on borrowing behavior. The result reveals that collateral was one of the major constraints. Land was the only collateral acceptable to institutional sources of credit. The tenants and share croppers were left out of the credit programmes. They concluded that the total amount borrowing model, initial liquid assets significantly impacted the amount of borrowing. Operational holding was significantly affecting the total house hold consumption expenditure.

Alexander Subbotin[2] **(2005)** says that the classic definition of credit rationing problem is that a farm cannot get credit at all or cannot get credit of the required size even in case it's ready to pay higher interest (a fair price considering associated risks), i.e. has no access to credit resources (Stiglitz, Weiss 1981). The study of credit rationing has a high practical value. First, credit rationing has a negative impact on agriculture's economic performance. According to Foltz (2003), losses are entailed by the fact that a farm is unable to optimally allocate resources in a short term (the profit-liquidity effect) and has to refrain from long-term investments in land and equipment since it cannot spread its expenditures over time (*investment demand effect*). However, it is important to consider that apparent deficit of credit may occur if farms are unable to achieve profitability sufficient for servicing credit and paying it back, i.e. are actually not ready to pay an equilibrium price for the credit. Some authors (Boucher, Carter, 2002) call this limitation connected with farm profitability *price rationing*. In this case, the shortage of circulating capital does not influence farm's allocation decisions. The classical non-price rationing as we have defined it above supposes that the possibility of getting credit for a farm first of all depends on its endowment and other factors but not on

[1]Akram Husain and Sial., (2008), "Agricultural Credit Constraints and Borrowing Behavior of Farmers in Rural Punjab", *European Journal of Scientific Research*, 27, 2, Pp. 294-304.

[2]Alexander Subbotin (2005), "Determinants of Credit Rationing for Corporate Farms in Russia", *Paper prepared for presentation at the XI Congress of the EAAE (European Association of Agricultural Economists), 'The Future of Rural Europe in the Global Agri-Food System', Copenhagen, Denmark, August 24-2.*

current investment opportunities. These five groups of factors affecting access of credit were operationalized by variables based on survey answers. Current repayment capacity was represented by sales revenue and profit margin (i.e., ratio of gross profit to sales revenue).

Sarap[1] (1990) made an elaborate enquiry to locate and analyse factors inhibiting small farmers' access to formal credit, including credit supply, bargaining strength, bureaucratic formalities, asset based lending policies, informal tenancy contracts, extended processing procedures and caste barriers. This study confirms a correlation between higher overall transaction costs and smaller farm size and also between arrearages and larger farm size. He noted that access to credit is far easier for some groups than for others then the question of small farmers effective access to these institutions is of crucial significance.

This study pointed out the reasons for additional formal credit:

1. Shift rural borrowing from informal money lenders to formal institutions.
2. Encourage increased borrowing for the exploitation of new technology, improved inputs etc.,
3. Provide modern mechanism for income transfer.
4. Lead to increased production and higher income for rural poor.

The main aim of the study is on the analysis of the factors limiting the access of small farmers to formal credit in a backward region of Orissa. The data used in the study are based on a field investigation in six villages of Sambalpur district of Orissa state in India. The field investigation was conducted during the year 1981-1982 and the data relate to the year 1980-1981. Data have been collected two distinct agro climatic zones. A stratified random sampling procedure was adopted to select a sample of 250 farmers from five size groups of holdings. The direct interview method is used to collect data with the help of suitably designed questionnaire. The empirical results are estimated through the PROBIT analysis. This paper finds that mere existence of credit institutions does not guarantee that small farmers will benefit from them. This paper also reveals that the dominance of large farmers in the decision making bodies of these institutions appear to have influenced the officials in the disbursal of credit infavour of large farmers and the dominant economic and social status also seem to have increased the probability of willful default of loans from these institutions.

---

[1]Kailas Sarap (1990), "Factors Affecting Small Farmers Access to Institutional Credit in Rural Orissa, India", *Development And Change,* 21, Pp. 281-307.

1.4. Importance of the Study

The overall mission statement of the economic policy may face several impediments when it enters the different stages to reach the ultimate needy. This study aims in analysing the issues relating to supply of agricultural credit at Macro, Meso (Bank) and Micro (Household) level. The overall economic policy of a country has collective influence on credit supply in general for productive purposes and for agriculture in particular at different phases of policy levels. The macro level determinants on the institutional credit flow to agriculture have occupied a crucial position in an emerging economy like India. The aggregate level of agricultural credit may well be considered as the combined result of macroeconomic policies which is transmitted through different channels. This study aims to analyse the relationship between macro level determinants and credit flow agriculture sector at aggregate level.

Credit delivery to the agriculture sector continues to be inadequate. The Indian banking system is still hesitant on various grounds to purvey credit to small and marginal farmers. Credit, as one of the critical non-land inputs, has two-dimensions from the viewpoint of its contribution to the augmentation of agricultural growth *viz.*, availability of credit (the quantum) and the distribution of credit (Ramesh Golait, 2007)[1]. This part focused only on commercial banks to reveal the effect of bank level variables in determining the agriculture credit policy. There is a tendency for formal credit to flow towards agriculturally more developed regions and to relatively larger farmers, leaving the backward regions and small farmers to the informal market. The main intention of this part is to study about dissimilarity in the access to credit and what makes some farm households to reach formal credit and others not. This part also touches on what basis bankers determine the credit limit to the borrower.

1.5. Scope of the Study

The macro level determinant on the commercial bank credit flow to agriculture has focused to the entire economy of India. The aggregate level of impact on commercial bank credit has been examined. The question of impact of macro level policy changes on agricultural credit by commercial banks are captured by the variables. The study took four kinds of variables like Output, Price, Policy and Aggregate Bank parameters. Based on annual data, the data base is build over the 40 years period from 1971 to 2011. Though, the year 1991 considered as the starting point of post reform and to avoid the paucity of data observations, the normalisation introduced without any structural break.

---

[1]Ramesh Golait (2007), "Current Issues in Agriculture Credit in India: An Assessment", *Reserve Bank of India Occasional Papers*, 28, 1, summer.

The effect of policy actions on commercial banks' balance sheet is often neglected into the background. The channels through which the policy actions get transmitted to the rest of the economy operated through the behaviour of the commercial banks.[1] The bank level analysis confined to 17 Public sector banks including SBI and its associates. The private sector banks comprise 10 and excluded the banks with lack of reporting of data. Foreign banks were excluded from the sample due to zero level focus on agriculture. The agricultural credit provided in the country through SCBs and RRBs have gone to states and reached the ultimate farmers. Since the banking sector reforms have not made any impact on the financial pattern of Co-operatives, the study is exclusively based on the finance provided by the Scheduled Commercial Banks to agricultural sector. The Scheduled Commercial Banks consist of State Bank of India and its Associates, Nationalised Banks, Foreign Banks, and Other Scheduled Commercial Banks.

In the case of micro level (households) analysis emphasis was given on the loan provided by formal institutions (Sahu,2002)[2]. The district level analysis has been done for the state of Tamil Nadu which is one of the top five states in terms of generation of gross domestic product. There is a need to look into the ground level credit flow to the different sectors in the state and mainly to neglected sectors like agricultural sector. The micro-level analysis has been carried in the specific context of Erode district, Tamil Nadu which is located in the western region of the state, and is known for agriculture and small business. For the micro level analysis, data from State Bank of India Gobichettipalayam Branch of Gobichettipalayam Block and State Bank of India Anthiyur Branch of Anthiyur Block and 505 farm households (falling within the service area of these bank branches) have been collected. Prior to that the results of the National Sample Survey on Situation Assessment of Farmers Indebtedness: NSS 59th Round also are discussed to get better insight.

1.6. Objectives of the Study

In light of these issues, the present study on credit flow to agriculture derives its relevance and has the following objectives.

1. To study the trends of agricultural credit by commercial banks before and after the introduction of the banking sector reforms;
2. To study the effect of Macro level variables on agricultural credit by commercial banks;

---

[1]Ray (2008), Op.Cit.

[2]Gagan Bihari Sahu (2002), *"Institutional Finance for Agriculture analysis at Macro and Micro levels"*, Unpublished Thesis, ISEC, Bangalore.

3. To analyse the effect of Bank level variables on agricultural credit by commercial banks and
4. To examine the effect of Micro level variables on agricultural credit by commercial banks

1.7. Hypotheses

The following hypotheses are tested in relation to the above objectives:

1. The agricultural credit by commercial banks may not differ with Macro level variables.
2. There is no significant difference between bank level characteristics and agricultural credit by commercial banks.
3. There is no significant difference between Micro level characteristics and agricultural credit by commercial banks.

1.8. Operational Definitions

Direct finance to Agriculture : Direct finance to agriculture shall include short, medium and long term loans given for agriculture and allied activities directly to individual farmers, Self-Help Groups (SHGs) or Joint Liability Groups (JLGs) of individual farmers without limit and to others (such as corporates, partnership firms and institutions) up to Rs. 20 lakh, for taking up agriculture/allied activities.

Indirect finance to Agriculture: Loans to entities covered in excess of Rs. 20 lakh in aggregate per borrower for agriculture and allied activities. In such cases, the entire amount outstanding shall be treated as indirect finance for agriculture. Loans to food and agro-based processing units with investments in plant and machinery up to Rs. 10 crore, undertaken by other than rural and semi-urban households.

Weaker Sections in Agriculture: Small and marginal farmers with land holding of 5 acres and less, and landless labourers, tenant farmers and share croppers come under this category. Loans are given to distressed urban/rural poor to prepay their debt to non-institutional lenders, against appropriate collateral or group security.

Household: A group of person normally living together and taking food from a common kitchen constitutes a household. By "normally" it is meant that temporary visitors are excluded while temporary stay-always are included. Thus, a son or a daughter residing in a hostel for studies is excluded from the household of his/her parents, but a resident employee or resident domestic servant or paying guest (but not just a tenant in the house) is included in the employer's/host's household.

Household size: The size of a household is the total number of persons, normally living in the household.

Farmer: For the purpose of this survey, a farmer is defined as "a person who operates on some land and is engaged in agricultural activities during the last 365 days". By agricultural activities, it is meant the cultivation of field crops and horticultural crops, growing of trees or plantations (such as rubber, cashew, coconut, pepper, coffee, tea, etc.), animal husbandry, poultry, fishery, piggery, bee-keeping, vermiculture, sericulture, etc.

Land possessed : Land possessed by the household is obtained by summing the land areas (in hectares) for plots owned, leased in and otherwise possessed by the household and then subtracting the land area for that leased out by the household.

Land owned: A plot of land is considered to be owned by the household if the right of permanent heritable possession, with or without the right to transfer the title, is vested in a member or members of the household. Land held in owner-like possession under long term lease or assignment is also considered as land owned.

Operational holding: An operational holding is a techno-economic unit constituted of all land that is used wholly or partly for agricultural production and is operated (directed/ managed) by one person alone or with assistance of others, without regard to title, size or location. The holding may consist of one or more parcels of land, provided that they are located within the country and that they form part of the same techno economic unit.

1.9. Methodology

The validity of any research is based on the systematic method of data collection and analysis. Both secondary and primary data were used for the present study. The secondary data were collected from authenticated publications. The primary data were collected from 500 respondents from Gobichettipalayam and Anthiyur blocks of Erode District.

Sources of Secondary Data

The data required for the study was taken from the various reports of Reserve Bank of India (RBI) and NABARD. The macro level variables and Bank level variables were collected from the annual reports of RBI, Handbook of Statistics on Indian Economy and Report on Currency and Finance. The macro level variables covered the years from 1971 to 2011. In order to evaluate the impact econometrically, there was a problem of paucity of observations. This said problem has been overcome by using the data, since 1971. This even precise the estimation and the results are robust in nature without any degree of freedom problem. The bank level variables pertaining to the period from 2001 to 2010 were included. The unbalanced panel data set based on annual data is developed for 27 banks and utilised with panel analysis for bank level variables.

The micro level variables pertaining to Tamil Nadu were taken through Situation Assessment Survey of Farmers Indebtedness of Farmer Households: NSS 59th Round (January–December 2003). The credit related data of Erode District were collected from the Annual Credit Plan of the Erode district from 2006-2011 with the intention to get better understanding of the study area.

Sources of Primary Data

The researcher has chosen State Bank of India in Erode District for the purpose of this study. The present study has used the length of canal used for irrigation as a proxy variable to identify the advanced and backward blocks[1]. The blocks namely Gobichettipalayam (from advanced group) and Anthiyur (backward group) were selected randomly. Further, SBI Gobichettipalayam branch of Gobichettipalayam Block and SBI Anthiyur branch of Anthiyur block (falling within the service area of these bank branches) were purposively selected.

With a view to give representation to different categories of farmers, 500 farmers who belong to the area of operation of SBI Gobichettipalayam and Anthiyur branch, and who have exclusively borrowed from the SBI, were selected for the study. While selecting the sample, care was taken to include the farmers who have not made any other investment previously, That is, the farmers who wanted the finance from the bank and made investment only in the agriculture were selected. The farmers who have availed finance one year before the study period was selected and farmers who were at the doorsteps of the bank for loan were also included. Representation was given to different categories of farmers like marginal, small and other categories of farmers.

1.10. Sampling Scheme

The main sketch of this study is to examine the formal credit for agricultural sector in India with specific reference to two blocks of Erode district of Tamil Nadu. The proportional study between the two blocks of Erode district were selected where the area of operation of SBI and who have exclusively borrowed from the SBI branch to understand and review institutional

---

[1]There is a tendency for formal credit to flow towards agriculturally more developed regions and to relatively larger farmers, leaving the backward regions and small farmers to the informal market.

credit at village level. The overall purpose of the work is to find how credit was rationed to the different category of farmers.

Selection of Sample Farmers and Collection of Data

Purposive sampling method was adopted for the selection of farmers from the State bank of India branch of Gobichettipalayam and Anthiyur. The farmers, who visited the Gobichettipalayam and Anthiyur branches during the period between August 2010 and December 2010, were considered as targeted population of sample farmers. A well-structured interview schedule in English was prepared and 550 bank customers of two branches in the ratio of 1:1 were interviewed. The residential addresses of sample farmers with mobile numbers were collected. Based on that the customers were interviewed and required data were collected from the sample farmers. On an average one hour has required to interview a farmer. Out of 550 sample farmers interviewed, 505 interview schedules were finalised. Owing to inconsistency, 500 sample farmers were considered for final analysis.

Table 1 shows the pattern of data collection and from the branches of SBI in Gobichettipalayam and Anthiyur.

Table 1.1: Pattern of Data Collection

Blocks	Interviewed	Valid	Used
Gobichettipalayam (A)	275	255	250
Anthiyur (B)	275	250	250
Total	550	505	500

1.11. Field Work and Collection of Data

Before the data collection, a model interview schedule was used for the purpose of pilot study. The schedule was pre-tested with the response obtained from 70 farmers. The feedback of the respondents was useful in carrying out a few corrections/modifications in the questions included earlier schedule.

1.12. Limitations of the Study

The study is subject to the following limitations.

1. Due to paucity of observations, the macro level variables are not grouped to pre and post reform period.
2. The study depended on 59th NSSO round to verify the overall indebtedness which pertains to the year of 2003. But the current round has already started during the month of January 2013, which may bring significant variations in the result.

3. In this study, some of the farmers may have failed to disclose their true income out of fear and confidentiality, which may have slightly the distorted the findings.
4. The study is restricted to a purposive sample of 500 respondents. Besides, the study was confined to Erode District only.
5. The study pertained to household level characteristics in selected SBI branches of the District which cannot be generalised for whole of the country for transmission of policy.
6. The conclusions would be based on the responses obtained from the respondents through interview schedule. Though utmost care has been taken to entice correct information, an element of subjectivity cannot be ruled out.

1.13. Chapter Scheme

Keeping in view of the objectives mentioned earlier, the present study was presented in six chapters along with tables and annexure to support the analysis and findings of the study. The interview schedule used to collect primary data and list of banks are appended at the end of the thesis.

Chapter I: Introduction and Design of the Study

This chapter contains introduction, statement of the problem, review of literature, scope of the study, objectives of the study, hypotheses, methodology, data processing and analysis, limitations and chapter scheme.

Chapter II: Trends of Agricultural Credit by Commercial Banks Before and After the Introduction of the Banking Sector Reforms

This chapter discusses the trends of agricultural credit by commercial banks before and after the introduction of banking sector reforms

Chapter III: Impact of Macro Level Variables on Agricultural Credit by Commercial Banks

This chapter contains an analysis of macro level variables on the agricultural credit by commercial banks.

Chapter IV: Impact of Bank Level Variables on Agricultural Credit by Commercial Banks

In this chapter, measurement and analysis of the impact of bank level variables on the agricultural credit by commercial banks are made.

Chapter V: Impact of Micro Level Variables on Agricultural Credit by Commercial Banks

This chapter analyses the effect of micro level variables on agricultural credit by commercial banks.

Chapter VI: Summary of Findings, Conclusion and Suggestions

The last chapter contains the summary of the findings that emerged from the analyses and offers necessary suggestions for improving the credit flow to agriculture with equity. This chapter ends with a suitable conclusion.

CHAPTER II

TRENDS OF INSTITUTIONAL CREDIT BEFORE AND AFTER THE REFORMS

2.1. Introduction

A developing economy faces many problems like poverty, scarcity of capital and there is dependence on agriculture and at the same time agriculture is not modernised. There is growing concern over the developing regional disparities in the countries; concern emanates both from the intellectual curiosity as well as political compulsions created by the development process. The commercial banks can work as catalytic agents of growth by following the right kind of policies in their working, depending upon the socio economic conditions prevailing in the country. The lending policy of the banks is purpose oriented that is banks serve production purpose in line with socially desired goals.[1] The commercial banks help the agricultural sector in number of ways. They open a network of branches in rural areas to provide agricultural credit. Commercial banks are the single most important source of institutional credit in India.

The banks are very important instruments of macroeconomic policy to stablise the economy. By controlling the volume of credit they are able to check both inflation and deflation effectively in the economy. In fact the central banks depend upon the commercial banks for success of its monetary policy, keeping in view the different requirements of developing economy. It is true that credit policy with regard to volume of and direction is subject to control by the central banking authority, still commercial banks can devise new way and means of moblising deposits and granting loans and thus can be innovative. Commercial banks have become a omnibus institution in the modern times to which people of varied interests look for help and success.

One of the major advantages of developmental credit policy, as enunciated at the time of bank nationalization was to seek to extend the reach of bank credit, both geographically and functionally. Geographically in the sense of covering the under banked regions of the country, especially the rural hinterland and functionally means extending credit to agriculture, small industry and to the self employed which were deemed to be important in terms of their contribution to national income growth and expansions of employment opportunities. Nationalization aimed at improving the economic status of those individual/sector which were

---

[1]Singh S. (1977), *"Performance Budgeting for Commercial Banks in India"*, the Macmillan Company of India Ltd., Delhi.

badly neglected in the pre nationalization era. The nationalized banks were further required to promote balanced economic development by removing regional imbalances. In the post nationalization era a significant move took place from class banking to mass banking. The main thrust of the commercial banks in this period (after nationalization and before financial sector reforms) was on social lending in order to fulfill the objectives of growth, equity, social justice and self reliance.[1] In spite of experiencing certain ups and downs the commercial banks have witnessed a phenomenal increase in India. Though at the time of independence there continued to be large number of non scheduled commercial banks yet, subsequently their number and their relative importance shrunk considerably.

2.2. Rationale of Banking Reforms

Though the branches, deposits and credit of the commercial banks registered an unperfected quantitative growth in post nationalization period yet , it was observed that over a period of time certain inherent weakness have cropped up in the Indian commercial banking system. It was observed that the banks have been irrationally following social objectives and economic objectives were thwarted in the dark. The poor generation of income profit over a period of time almost made the baking institutions unviable in nature. There were number of reasons responsible for this financial chaos in the commercial banks, which for a longer period of time had been affecting the overall business and earning capacity of banks. For example the high rate of SLR and CRR in the past to be a large extent reduced the business capacity of the commercial banks. The banks were statutorily required to keep 15 percentage of their aggregate demand and time liabilities as cash reserve ratio with the apex central bank. Besides it, they were also required to invest 38.5 percentage of the net demand and time liabilities as SLR in approved government securities. Apart from this, banks were further required to invest 10 percentage of total demand and time liabilities accumulated the banking system during a specific period, as impounded reserve. This implies that the banking system was called upon to divert 63.5 percentage of their total deposit resources in meeting statutory obligations. This direct investment programme had seriously affected the resources position of the banks. As a result of these statutory provisions the banks were left with only 36.5 percentage of aggregate deposit resources to look into the interest of other competing sectors.[2] Because of these investments, banks earned very little rate of interest, which led to poor profit earnings by the banks.

[1]Report of the Banking Commission, 1972.

[2]Reserve Bank of India (1991): *Report of the Committee on the Financial System*, (chaired by M. Narasimham)

The poor performance of several corporations and delay in repayment of loans by them further affected the income earning capacity of the banks. These investments not only reduced the availability of funds in the hands of banks but also failed to meet the growing needs of the borrowers engaged in the productive activities. Very often the central bank's decision to reduce interest rate on loans in harmony with the lower deposit rates also affected the income earnings capacity of the banks.[1] The uncompetitive environment, operating inflexibility, managerial weakness and more importantly lack of autonomy in decisions making have been the major reasons of the poor performance of the public sector banks.[2]

2.3. The Directed Credit Programmes and Banking Reforms

The implementation of directed credit programme assigned by the government to the public sector banks is held as the other most important factor responsible, for making the banking system inefficient and vulnerable. Under DCP, banks are called upon to channelize 40 percentage of total bank credit in favour of the targeted priority sectors, which were neglected badly in the pre nationalization period. They were required to attain this target by the year 1985. With this broad allocation framework, the banks are also supposed to see that the sub sectors of the economy get their due share of credit. Banks are directly to supply 16 percentage of total priority sectors advances in favour of agriculture and allied activities. They are also required to channelize the ten percentage of the total priority sector finance in favour small scale industries. The banks are also required to meet the credit needs of certain target groups under various beneficiary schemes like IRDP, DRI, and NREP etc. The rate of interest on priority sector lending is kept artificially low to enable the large number of borrowers to avail such loans. The losses in income from such sectors are compensated by charging higher rate of interests from the borrowers, belonging to non priority and non food sectors. This cross subsidization of loans was thought to be helpful for banks in planning their credit allocation. However, this system could not ensure higher and smooth earnings for the banks. It is observed that due to directed credit programme also, resources available with the banking sector for supplying funds to sectors like plantation, large scale and medium scale industries, trade and commercial occupations have remained very low. This resulted in lopsidedness in the portfolio of loan operations, affecting both efficiency and productivity of the banks.[3]

---

[1]Reserve Bank of India (2004): *Report of the Advisory Committee on Flow of Credit to agriculture and Related Activities.*

[2]Reserve Bank of India (1989): *A Review of Agricultural Credit System in India.*

[3]Rangarajan C. (1999), "Rationale of Reforms in the Financial Sector", *The Indian Economic Journal*, 46, 3, Pp. 8-10.

In fact the priority sector lending has become a major reason of financial strain from the commercial banks because of the poor recovery rate also. The poor recoveries of loans, particularly the agricultural loans have seriously aggravated the problem of NPAs and have put a question mark on the issue of sustainability of the commercial banks as such. Recovery of direct agricultural loans, which stood at 56.8 percentage in 1988, declined to 46.8 percentage in 1990. Likewise, considerable amount of bank funds was further locked in small-scale industries too owing to chronic sickness of these units. According to RBI sources at the end of September 1989, there were 1.86 lakh sick units involving bank finance to the tune of Rs.2243 crores. Thus, on the one hand, banks are losing considerable amount on account of subsidized rate of interest charged on priority sector lending, and on the other hand. poor recovery of loans and mounting over-dues have further reduced the income generation capacity of the banks. The levels of NPAs have been rising at a very high rate and they touched a staggering figure of Rs.43,577 crores in the year'1988. The list of banks with massive NPA is led by State Bank of India group with Rs.14,367 crores and the other public sector banks account for Rs.29,207 crores.

2.4. Narasimham Committee on Banking Reforms

The second Banking Sector Reforms Committee under the Chairmanship of M.Narashimham to review the progress in the banking sector reforms and make suitable recommendations was set up on 19th December 1997[1] and this time it was called the committee on the Banking Sector Reforms. The Committee was asked to review the progress of banking sector reforms particularly with the reference to the recommendations made by the Narasimham Committee (1), and to chart out a programme on banking sector reforms necessary to strengthen the India's banking system which can make it internationally competitive.

The Narasimham Committee on the Banking Sector Reforms submitted its reports to the Government in April 1998. This covered the entire gamut of issues, ranging from capital adequacy, bank mergers, and the creation of global- sized banks, recasting bank boards and revamping bank legislation. However, detailed recommendations with respect to the banking policy, institutional, supervisory and technological dimensions were also given by it. While assessing the Capital Adequacy Ratio, the Committee felt that the market risks should be taken into consideration. It was realized that there was a need for increasing risk weight of investment in government securities. The risk weight to advances under the government guarantee also should be the same as for other advances. More risk weight, according to the

---

[1]Report of the Narashimham Committee (2) (1998), *"On the Banking Sector Forms"*, Nabhi Publications, New Delhi.

Committee, on foreign exchange open credit limit risks should be integrated into calculation on the risk weight assets and should carry 100 percentage weight. The committee also realised that the Capital Adequacy has to be increased from the existing level of 8 percentage to 10 percentage in a phased manner, viz., 9 percentage by 2000 and 10 percentage by 2002. The RBI should have the freedom to ask specific banks to increase the Capital Adequacy for a specific bank, provided the risk profile of the given bank requires such change in the capital adequacy norms. The committee also suggested higher capital adequacy requirements for banks and the setting up of an Asset Reconstruction Fund to take over the bad debt of the banks.

According to the Committee, for increasing the capital adequacy of PSBs there exist only two channels, viz., The Government of India and Capital market. The Committee observed that Rs.20,000 crores or more were pumped in the banks as re-capitalisation which enabled banks to make provision for bad and doubtful debts. The Committee felt that such alternative for strengthening the banks could not be a sustainable source. Therefore, the Committee was not in favour of efforts of the Indian Government to provide funds from budget as re-capitalisation of banks. The Committee felt that an asset should be classified as a doubtful asset if it is in the sub-standard category for 18 months in the first instance and eventually for 12 months. It recommended further that after 12 months, if assets still do not improve, they should also be identified as losses but not written off. Such norms, according to the Committee, should be regarded as minimum and brought into force in a phased manner. It recommended that there should be an independent loan review mechanism especially for large borrower accounts and systems to identify potential NPAs.

As far as the management of NPAs is concerned, the Committee observed that the NPAs figures do not include advances covered by the government guarantee and which have turned sticky. Similar loans without such guarantee are being classified as NPA. The committee felt that such advances even though they are covered by the guarantee of the government should be classified as NPA. And these should be shown separately in the balance sheets of banks to facilitate fuller disclosure and greater transparency of operations.

The Committee was of the view that the figures relating to NPAs are being artificially reduced by the banks and this practice should not be permitted by rescheduling the loan. The Committee has suggested that the banks with high NPAs level have two alternatives. The first alternative is to create Accrued Rate of Credit (ARC). Secondly, all loans in doubtful and loss categories should be identified and their realizable value should be determined. These assets should be transferred to an ARC, which would issue Non Performing Assets (NPAs) swap bonds. The other alternative could be to enable banks in the difficulty to issue bonds which could be from the part of Tier-II capital, backed by Government guarantee to make these instruments eligible for SLR investment by banks. In the case of Directed Credit, the Committee felt that the share of priority sector in the bank credit has to be reduced from the existing level of 40 percentage to 10 percentage and there is a need for redefining the concept of priority sector should be totally eliminated and interest rate on loans under Rs.2 lakh should be de-regularised for scheduled commercial banks. Further, as far as the prudential norms are concerned, it was suggested that with regard to the income recognition, when interest on installment of principal is not paid within 180 days, income stops accruing in India, should be reduced to 90 days in the phased manners by 2002. As an incentive to make specific provisions, there should be some tax deductions for such provisioning". [1]

The committee has taken the note of the twin phenomena of consolidation and convergence, with which the financial system IS experiencing globally. In India also, the committee felt that banks and Development Financial Institutions (DFIs) are moving closer to each other in the scope of their activities. The committee observed that DFIs should over a period of time convert themselves into the banks, so that in future, there would be only two types of financial intermediaries, viz., banks and non-banks in India. The committee made it very much clear that if the given DFIs are not taking banking license from the RBI, in the stipulated time frame, it should be treated as Non-Banking Financial Corporation (NBFCs). The Committee opined that as long as the directed credit is in practice special formula could be worked out for the DFIs, which are converted into the banks.

It also recommended the adaptation of the concept of narrow banking to rehabilitate the weak banks. Narrow banking implies that the weak banks place their funds only in the short term and attempt to match their demand deposits by safe liquid assets. In case the concept of narrow banking is found to be non-applicable to rehabilitate weak banks, the issue of closure should be examined, according to the committee. The committee strongly argued that the Government ownership and management of banks does not enhance autonomy and flexibility in the working of public sector banks. In this connection, the Committee has recommended a review of the functions of boards so that the bank board remains responsible for enhancing share holder value through formulation of corporate strategy.

In order to have a strong banking system, the committee recommended the mergers of weak bankers with the strong banks. However, the committee cautioned that this might have negative impact on the asset quality of the stronger banks. It observed that the merger of PSBs

[1]Report of the Narashimham Committee (2) (1998), ibid.

should emanate from the management of the banks with the government as the common shareholder playing a supportive role. Mergers should not be seen as a means of bailing out weak banks. Such mergers however can be worthwhile if they lead to rationalization of work force and branch network. If the mergers between the banks and the financial institutions are to take place it should be based on synergies, location, business specific complementarities of the institutions concerned and must obviously, make sound commercial scene.

Further, it was suggested that the no-bank parties be provided free access to bill rediscounts, Commercial Papers, Certificates of Deposits, Treasury Bills and Money Market Mutual Funds. The need to change the deposit insurance scheme based on CAMEL rating awarded by the RBI to the respective banks was emphasized. The committee recommended that the minimum shareholding by the Government of India, RBI in the equity of nationalized banks and State Bank of India should be brought down to 33 percentage. In a nutshell, the recommendations of the Committee envisage far reaching changes in the financial environment in general and banking environment in particular. It was expected that the proposed financial sector reforms would help to promote the development of rural sector in the economy.

2.5. Trends of Institutional Credit before and After the Reforms

The government of India accepted almost all the major recommendations of Narasimham Committee and started implementing them straight away despite stiff opposition from bank unions and political parties in the country. As a result of the process of the Banking Sector Reforms, the Statutory Liquidity Ratio (SLR) on incremental net demand and time liabilities has been reduced from 38.5 percentage to 25 percentage. Similarly, SLR on outstanding net domestic demand and time liabilities, have also been reduced gradually from 38.5 percentage in the year 1992, to 27 percentage in March 1997 and further to 25 percentage in October 1997. This is the minimum stipulated under the section 24 of the Banking Regulation Act, 1949.

Originally it was the intention of the RBI to bring down the Cash Reserve Ratio (CRR) from the statutory 15 percentage and in fact it was brought down to 14 percentage in May 1993. At the same time, the incremental CRR of 10 percentage was also abolished. When conditions eased and the money growth started slowing down during 1995-96, 'the RBI reduce CRR gradually from 15 percentage in 1992 to 10 percentage by March 1997. The purpose of reducing CRR was to release funds locked up with RBI for lending to the industrial and other sectors, which were starved of bank credit. Similarly, in view of the reforms, the interest rate slabs were gradually reduced from 20 to 2 by 1994-95. The important changes in interest rate since 1991-92 are, the interest rates on domestic term deposits above one year and non-residential non-repairable rupee deposits have been decontrolled, the prime lending rate of SBI and most other banks on general advances of over rupees 2lakhs has been reduced. In addition to it, the rate of interest on bank loans above two lakhs too has been fully de-controlled.

In view of the banking sector reforms, scheduled commercial banks have now been given freedom to open new branches and upgrade extension counters, after satisfying the capital adequacy norms and the prudential accounting standards. They are also permitted to close non viable branches other than in rural areas. The bank lending norms have been liberalized and the banks have been made free to decide levels of holding of individual items, of inventories and receivables. Because of the implementation of the recommendations of the Banking Sector Reforms the numbers of the private and foreign banks have increased many folds during the late nineties. The details regarding the share of institutional credit to agriculture out of total credit level are given below.

Table 2.1: Trends of Commercial Bank Credit to Agriculture before Reforms

(Amount in Rs Crore)

Year	Direct (i)	Indirect (ii)	Total (iii)	Total Credit (iv)	Percentage (i) to (iii)	Percentage (ii) to (iii)	Percentage (iii) to (iv)
1973	40943	16222	57165	633347	71.62	28.38	9.03
1974	53765	17109	70874	799906	75.86	24.14	8.86
1975	65791	31079	96870	901102	67.92	32.08	10.75
1976	88834	32588	121422	1167831	73.16	26.84	10.4
1977	109957	29985	139942	1345699	78.57	21.43	10.4
1978	140503	55595	196098	1596113	71.65	28.35	12.29
1979	194574	57540	252114	1916264	77.18	22.82	13.16
1980	241779	73425	315204	2131161	76.71	23.29	14.79
1981	303267	112755	416022	2487476	72.9	27.1	16.72
1982	380306	127288	507594	2959038	74.92	25.08	17.15
1983	425964	152635	578599	3502025	73.62	26.38	16.52
1984	614351	151125	765477	4332570	80.26	19.74	17.67
1985	733892	148132	882024	4999457	83.21	16.79	17.64
1986	831223	145804	977027	5618178	85.08	14.92	17.39
1987	931822	170053	1101875	6372739	84.57	15.43	17.29
1988	1079266	172295	1251561	7128468	86.23	13.77	17.56
1989	1338978	187602	1526580	8802707	87.71	12.29	17.34
1990	1443532	219075	1662607	10431193	86.82	13.18	15.94

Source: RBI's Basic Statistical Returns of Scheduled Commercial Banks in India, various issues.

Table 2.1 illustrates the quantum of loans disbursed by commercial banks in India prior to reform period. The share of credit by commercial banks to agriculture considerably occupies a position on the institutional credit flow to the total economy. The share has raised from 9 percentage to 17 percentage during the period from 1973 to 1989. The year 1990, regarded as the starting point of the economic reforms, posted the declining trend of commercial bank credit flow to agriculture. .

Table 2.2: Trends of Commercial Bank Credit to Agriculture after Reforms

(Amount in Rs Crore)

Year	Direct(i)	Indirect (ii)	Total (iii)	Total Credit (iv)	Percentage (i) to (iii)	Percentage (ii) to (iii)	Percentage (iii) to (iv)
1991	1597132	260206	1857338	12420293	85.99	14.01	14.95
1992	1783555	240208	2023764	13670582	88.13	11.87	14.8
1993	1949350	256672	2206022	16246729	88.36	11.64	13.58
1994	1966974	320312	2287287	17589127	86	14	13
1995	2142051	352750	2494802	21093912	85.86	14.14	11.83
1996	2455613	425282	2880896	25469211	85.24	14.76	11.31
1997	2721736	441680	3163415	28437330	86.04	13.96	11.12
1998	3050890	475362	3526252	32994444	86.52	13.48	13.69
1999	3394114	694812	4088926	32994444	83.01	16.99	12.39
2000	3856079	707748	4563827	46008068	84.49	15.51	9.92
2001	4342026	831008	5173035	53843379	83.94	16.06	9.61
2002	4743042	1657812	6400855	65599308	74.1	25.9	9.76
2003	5905756	1687766	7593522	75596882	77.77	22.23	10.04
2004	7009873	2614631	9624504	88031203	72.83	27.17	10.93
2005	9463537	2974950	12438487	115246793	76.08	23.92	10.79

Source: RBI's Basic Statistical Returns of Scheduled Commercial Banks in India, various issues.

Table 2.2 demonstrates the loans disbursed by commercial banks in India after the reform period. The place of commercial banks credit to agriculture displays mixed results after the reform years. It clearly shows the governments' insignificant approach towards agriculture sector. The share has reduced from 14.95 percentage to 10.79 percentage during the period from 1991 to 2005. The other interesting trend on agriculture credit is that, the share of indirect finance to total agriculture credit is on a declining due to widening of definition on agricultural credit policies.

Table 2.3: Share of Institutional Agencies in Outstanding Cash Debt

States	1971 (NSS 26th round)	1981 (NSS 37th round)	1991 (NSS 48th round)	2002 (NSS 59th round)
Andhra Pradesh	14	41	34	27
Bihar	11	47	73	37
Gujarat	47	70	75	67
Haryana	26	76	73	50
Karnataka	30	78	78	67
Kerala	44	79	92	81
Madhya Pradesh	32	66	73	59
Orissa	30	81	80	74
Punjab	36	74	79	56
Rajasthan	9	41	40	3
Tamil Nadu	22	44	58	47
Uttar Pradesh	23	55	69	56
West Bengal	31	66	82	68
All India	29	61	64	57

Source: NSSO (2005b, Report 501, Statement 7, p.27)

The share of institutional credit outstanding by commercial banks in India before and after the reform period is depicted in Table 2.3. This is the evidence generated by National Sample Survey on agricultural indebtedness. This survey covered the entire India to find out whether credit reaches to the bottom of the farmers or not. From the table, it is clear that the share of institutional credit displayed an increasing trend from the year 1971 to 1991 i.e. prior to reforms. The latest 59th round on farmers' situation assessment conveys that the share of institutional credit to agriculture is 57 percentage. This proves that the commercial banks move to new areas other than agriculture in its priority credit.

2.6. Conclusion

The increase in the supply of credit to agriculture has been claimed to be one of the most significant achievements in the agricultural sector after the formation of the new government in 2004. The extent of revival of credit flow to agriculture in the 2000s would have been far less impressive in the absence of a sharp growth in indirect finance to agriculture.[1] It is by now well documented that the trends that emerged in India in the 1990s with respect to the supply

[1]Pallavi Chavan (2005), "How 'Inclusive' Are Banks under Financial Liberalisation?", *Economic & Political Weekly*, pp. 4647-49.

of rural credit in general, and agricultural credit in particular, were disturbing. In the 1990s, there was (a) large-scale closure of commercial bank branches in rural areas; (b) a widening of interstate inequalities in credit provision, and a fall in the proportion of bank credit directed towards regions, where banking was historically underdeveloped; (c) a sharp fall in the growth of credit flow to agriculture; (d) increased sidelining of small and marginal farmers in the supply of agricultural credit; (e) increased exclusion of the disadvantaged and dispossessed sections of the population from the formal financial system; and (f) strengthening of the hold of moneylenders on rural debt portfolios.[1] It is concluded that the there is a sharp decline in agriculture credit after reforms especially direct finance to agriculture.

[1]Ramachandran, and Madhura Swaminathan (eds) (2004), *"Financial Liberalisation and Rural Credit in India"*, Tulika Books, New Delhi.

CHAPTER III

MACRO LEVEL VARIABLES AND AGRICULTURAL CREDIT BY COMMERCIAL BANKS

3.1. Introduction

The macro level determinants on the institutional credit flow to agriculture have occupied a crucial position in an emerging economy like India. The aggregate level of agricultural credit may well be considered as the combined result of macroeconomic policies which is transmitted through different channels. Macroeconomic models evolve over time due to various externalities. Some of the macroeconomic models of the Indian economy are focusing on output, the fiscal sector and external sector. A survey of the existing macro models indicates that while there is a harmony on certain aspects of the economy, there are other areas that are less than fully understood. Depending on their objective and focus, different models have adopted different levels of disaggregation at the sector levels. Though there are variations in general, economic activities have been classified into four sectors, such as agriculture, manufacturing, service and public administration. Intra-sectoral disaggregation levels have also differed from model to model depending on the objective of the model builder. The main intention of this chapter is to study the response of institutional credit to macroeconomic characteristics. The macro level determinants play an important role in driving the flow of institutional credit to agriculture and priority sector as well. The policy on agricultural finance at macro level primarily concerns with the levels of credit flow to agriculture, terms and conditions under which it made available. Allocation of credit between sub-sectors (production and investment) to the needy farmers, encouraging them to adopt new agricultural technology and pre and post appraisal of loan disbursement etc.[1].

The economic reforms did not include any specific package for agriculture. Rather, the presumption was that freeing agricultural markets and liberalising external trade in agricultural commodities would provide price incentives leading to enhanced investment and output in that sector. However, the pattern of structural adjustment and the government's macro-economic strategy since 1991 have actually been associated with a reduced rate of overall agricultural growth declines in per capital food grain output and inadequate

[1]Sahu (2007), Op.Cit., Pp. 664-678.

employment generation.[1] Financial liberalisation measures, including reducing priority sector lending by banks, have effectively reduced the availability of rural credit and thus reduced farm investment, especially by smaller farmers.

Initially, the reforms focused mainly on the industrial and financial sectors and agriculture was mostly kept outside the scope of reforms. However, the agriculture sector be fitted indirectly from reforms due to exchange rate policy and improvements in terms of trade.[2] In a country with diverse agro-climatic, socio-economic and institutional circumstances, the need, nature and impact of input-output market reforms would differ across regions. Development of agricultural sector is critically dependent on the use of modern input such as fertilisers, seeds, plant propagation material, agricultural chemicals and the availability of credit to purchase these and other inputs. There is a need to ensure adequate and timely supply of all these inputs.

Economic growth is always parallel to the prevailing macroeconomic conditions. An advantageous macroeconomic environment is necessary for rapid economic growth. Macroeconomic instability, characterised by high rates of inflation, a fragile foreign exchange position, high rates of interest, increases uncertainty for any investor or producer and hence slows down economic growth. Besides, these direct indicators, macroeconomic instability may also be indicated by fiscal imbalance and external current account imbalance, especially when prices are under administrative controls. An underlying assumption in these arguments is that production sectors are influenced by macroeconomic conditions. Any attempt to examine this reposition will require identification of the indicators of macroeconomic conditions and of the performance of the sectors.[3]

Committee on the Financial Sector Reform (CFSR) formed by Rahuram Rajan intensively discussed about the macroeconomic framework. One cannot agree more with the CFSR on the need for a disciplined and predictable monetary, fiscal and debt management policies for the success of financial sector reforms and, in turn, the critical importance of a well functioning financial system for macroeconomic stability. There cannot be two opinions on the need for financial inclusion. The CFSR recommends measures for financial inclusion, recognising that

---

[1]Chand Ramesh, Raju S.S. and L.M.Pandey (2007), Op.Cit, Pp. 2528-33.

[2]Dholakia Bakul H. (1997), "Impact of Economic Liberalisation on the growth on Indian Agriculture, *Agricultural Development Paradigm for the Ninth Plan under New Economic Environment*, Oxford and IBH Publishing Company, Newdelhi.

[3]Shashanka Bide, R. Meeenashi and Vani B.P. (2005), "Do macro economic conditions matter for agriculture? The Indian Experience", Working Paper No. 162, ISEC.

access to credit rather than cost of credit matters for the nearly three-quarter of poor households who are outside the purview of banking in India. This is true when the report acknowledges that the poor engages in credit dealings with the indigenous moneylenders at an exorbitant interest rate, which is well above the mandated lending rate for banks. While advocating GenNext reforms, the CFSR emphasises the significance of a well-functioning regulatory mechanism and for establishing new regulatory institutions and new legislative fiats for fixing the financial sector.[1]

Financial liberalisation is one of the reforms released to the financial sector where banking sector plays an important role. Financial liberalisation is to represent a clear and explicit reversal of the policy of social and development banking. It is well known that the burden of indebtedness in rural India is very great despite major structural changes in credit institutions and forms of rural credit in the post-independence period. The exploitation of the rural masses in the credit market is one of the most pervasive and persistent features of rural life in India. There are four major problems with respect to the supply of credit to the rural India namely inadequate supply of formal credit, imperfect rural credit market, public policy and exploitation of borrowers.[2]

The agricultural sector in India has been important from a policy perspective for several reasons. Even from the point of view of accelerating economic growth, transition from an agrarian economy to an industrial or modern economy would depend on how well the agricultural sector enables this transition. Therefore, besides the concerns relating to employment and poverty alleviation, the performance of agriculture is of policy interest from the viewpoint of accelerating economic growth as well. The general belief is that overall macroeconomic policies have little effect on the agricultural sector and we need sector-specific policies to boost this primary sector of the economy. The macroeconomic environment may also have non-trivial effects on the agricultural sector. It is necessary to examine this hypothesis more rigorously, as if it does influence agricultural performance, and to understand the significance of this impact in designing policies for agriculture.[3] The primary purpose of this chapter is to determine the relationship between macro economic variables and agricultural credit by commercial banks.

[1]Chakraborthy Lakha (2008), "Analysing Rahuramrajan committee report on financial sector reforms", *Economic and Political Weekly*, 43, Pp. 11-14.

[2]Ramachandran and Vikas Jaiswal (2009), "The Impact of Liberlisation and Globalization on India's Agrarian Economy, *Global Labour Journal*, 1,1, Special Issue.

[3]Shashanka Bide, Meeenashi and Vani (2005), Op.Cit.

3.2. Theoretical Underpinning on Macro Policies and Agriculture

Mahendra Dev (2009)[1] clearly noted that there is a need to have pro-agriculture macro policies. The experience in several countries during the reform period shows that public expenditure as percentage of GDP is low and declining. As a result, Public investment in the rural development has declined sharply in most of the Asian countries. Consequently, agricultural growth slowed down in most countries during the 1990s. The average annual rate of growth of gross capital formation also slowed down in many countries. Trade liberalisation has been associated with increased ratio of trade to GDP, improved export performance, and diversification towards manufactured exports. However, linkages to employment are not so well established. Financial sector has historically had an urban bias. On balance, the macro policies have not been pro-employment and pro-poor in the post-reform period in many developing countries, including India. Therefore, there is a need to have pro-poor macro policies.

Most model builders for instance have disaggregated the agriculture into food grains and non-food grains sector. Ahluwalila and Rangarajan (1986)[2] differentiated between food grains and non-food grains sector. The agriculture sector is the primary supplier of raw materials and food grains for the Indian economy. In most of the models, agriculture sector is taken to be supply determined. The total output in this sector is determined given technology, by natural resources particularly land area, water, fertiliser and capital stock. All these variables are expected to affect the production positively. The provision of this input is important because credit or loanable fund is viewed as more than just another resource such as labour, land, equipment and raw materials. Eminent economists pointed out that farm credit is not only required by the limitation of self-finance but also uncertainty pertaining to the level of farm inputs and output and the time lag between input and output. There is a need for institutional finance in agriculture development where commercial banks take the lead to fulfill the requirements. In terms of fiscal policy, pro-poor approach involves increasing tax/GDP ratio, improving expenditures on agriculture and rural development, infrastructure and other capital expenditures. Pro- poor monetary and financial liberalisation policies should improve access to agricultural credit of small and marginal farmers and also to the informal sector.

---

[1]Mahendra dev (2009), "Challenges for Revival of Indian Agriculture", *Agricultural Economics Research Review*, 22, Pp. 21-45.

[2]Ahluwalia and Rangarajan (1986): '*Agriculture and Industry: A study of Linkages the Indian Experience*', mimeo, World Economic Congress of International Association, December.

In the case of India, the introduction of banking sector reforms discourage the directed credit after 1991 and wider the definition for the directed credit policies. There was a revival of agricultural credit, which however was mainly owing to an increase in indirect finance and a series of changes in the definition of "agricultural credit".[1] The policy instruments to achieve these objectives were to be: first, extending the geographical and functional reach of the formal sector; second, directed lending; and third, concessional or subsidised credit.[2]

There is little quarrel among economists on the effect that this flow of credit had on agricultural growth. The regulations on banking and the promotional role of the government were premised on the recognition that rural credit markets are deeply imperfect. The social and developing banking policy consciously mopped up surplus- savings from richer rural areas as deposits and diverted them as loans to savings-deficient areas.[3] The common undertaking of the economic policy may face several barriers when it enters the different stages to reach the ultimate needy. The main aim of this section is to study the inter-linkage between the institutional credit to agriculture and the macro economic variables. To fulfill our objective, the reseearcher has developed a model by considering several theories. This study focuses only on commercial banks and it uses time series econometric analysis to estimate the relationship.

3.3. Selection of Variables for the Analysis

India is a country exposed to major level of change in macroeconomic policies in the 1990s due to its opening up of economy to the rest countries. These considerable changes at the macroeconomic level were alteration in the fiscal and financial sectors, trade and investment policies. It has been argued that agriculture was insulated and only indirectly affected by these reforms. The industrial sector was most affected directly by the removal of the production licensing system enforced through control over new investments. Changes in the financial sector including exchange rate policies and attempts to stabilize fiscal imbalance, however, can be expected to have an impact across all the sectors. This section tries to seek answer for the question how important this impact to agriculture? i.e. output, prices, policy actions and balance sheet variables.[4] At wider economy level, there are many indicators to represent the

[1]Ramakumar, and Chavan, Pallavi (2007), "Revival of Agricultural Credit in the 2000s: An Explanation", *Economic and Political Weekly*, 42 (52), December 29, Pp. 57-63.

[2]Rangarajan, (1996): "*Agricultural Growth and Industrial Performance in India*", Research Report 33, International Food Policy Research Institute, October.

[3]Ramachandran, and Swaminathan, Madhura (eds.) (2005), *Financial Liberalisation and Rural Credit in India*, Tulika Books, New Delhi.

[4]Ray Partha (2008), "*Commercial Banks and Monetary Policy in India*", Academic Foundation.

macroeconomic conditions. This study classifies the macroeconomic conditions into different sectors. This study has four broad categories of variables in the empirical investigation i.e. output, prices, policy actions and balance sheet variables.

The agricultural credit variables considered in this study are: Direct Finance to Agriculture, Indirect Finance to Agriculture, Total Credit to Agriculture and Outstanding credit to agriculture. This study has utilized the VAR and the impulse response functions in quantifying the impact of macroeconomic factors on institutional credit flow to agriculture. Annual data for the period 1970-71 to 2010-11 are used for the analysis. This period covers a variety of experiences both in macroeconomic conditions, agricultural performance and policies.

Output Indicators($AGDP_t$)

The standard output indicator, namely Agricultural GDP is available only at a yearly interval in India. The acceleration of GDP growth during the last decade was accompanied by a significant moderation in volatility, especially in industry and service sectors. The structure of domestic output has shifted from industry to the service sector where initially contributed much by the agriculture sector. Agriculture GDP is considered as one of the indicators of output of agricultural sector.[1]

Price Indicators (WPI_t)

Since in the Indian context there is no grand consumer price index covering all sections of population, the researcher had to use Wholesale Price Index (WPI) for this purpose. In practical, WPI does not include traders' margin and conceptually it stands midway between an index for producer's price and the same for whole sale price. This is also called as inflation situation in a country[2].

Policy Indicators

This study has used CRR and SLR as policy variables used by central banks to control economic fluctuations particularly through credit supply.

Investment in Government Securities (SLR_t)

The balance sheet of any commercial banking institution clearly portrays the sources and uses of funds. There are two major considerations that weight with a bank in deciding the composition of assets. If we look commercial banking system as a business enterprise, there is

[1]Ray Partha (2008), Op.Cit.

[2]Shashanka Bide, Meeenashi and Vani (2005), Op.Cit

a need for banks to generate enough returns on its assets so that after paying interest on deposits it has attracted, it makes a profit. If a bank maintains its entire amount in raw cash, it will be liquid and safe but it lacks in yielding returns. A bank will always try to minimize the holding of cash as, it earns no profit. However, in order to protect itself in situations of sudden demand of cash, a bank usually keeps a certain amount of funds as investment in government securities which can be easily converted into cash. Investments in government securities occupy an important position in situations when the absence of legal requirements will constitute an important part of the assets of a commercial bank. Sahu (2002) quoted that in a regulated lending system, given interest rate and default risk, bankers may be more interested in increasing the proportion of investment in securities out of total deposits which may leave the banks with less loanable funds. It may adversely affect the channelization of credit to different sectors of the economy in general and agriculture in particular.[1]

Cash Reserve Ratio (CRR_t)

The instruments of credit control can be broadly divided in to two categories- general and selective. The general instruments are intended to regulate the total volume of credit. The selective instruments are used to regulate the purpose for which the credit is generated by the commercial banks. RBI has progressively raised the CRR throughout the 1970's and 1980's in order to neutralize the monetary impact of the monetization of the fiscal deficit.

Banking Variables

This study considers three banking aggregate variables viz., aggregate deposits, Credit by Cooperatives and RRBs and Rural coverage of banks.

Aggregate Deposits (AD_t)

The commercial banking system is considered to be one of the important systems in performing the major function of providing a link between those who have surplus fund and who are in need of funds. In the process, these institutions help to mobilize more resources and to allocate them more efficiently. In the presence of commercial banking system, a needy can easily access to financial resources. The aggregate deposits that kept with the commercial banks become an important determinant in providing loan to different sectors. Some economists argue that both demand and time deposits are also considered as money due to its easy convertibility. There is a positive association between dispersal of credit and amount of

[1]Gagan Bihari Sahu (2002), *"Institutional Finance for Agriculture analysis at Macro and Micro levels"*, Unpublished Theis, ISEC, Bangalore.

deposits with the commercial banks. The expansion of deposits occurs through expansion of credit as in the case of all financial institutions, the extent of lending will depend on the marginal cost of borrowing and the marginal return on lending. The expansion of deposits has resulted in expansion of lending by keeping only a fraction of the deposits in cash. The amount of cash that have to maintain against the deposits sets a limit on credit and deposit expansion- the larger the proportion of deposits to be kept in the form of cash, the lower the expansion of credit.

Credit by Cooperatives and RRBs ($CRRBL_t$)

Credit institutions including cooperatives and Regional Rural Banks play an important role in attracting funds from the public by inviting deposits. Economic units including farms, getting funds from those institutions to fulfill their need. In an emerging economy, one particular economic unit may not be over focused. Here, if the agriculture credit share is occupied by RRBs means there is a diversion of credit from commercial banks from the agriculture sector. An increase in the total agricultural credit supplied by other than commercial banks may reduce the extent of credit supplied by commercial banks. Banking institutions do always maintain mutual understanding in allocating the credit to the different sectors otherwise it resulted in over injection of resources in one sector.

Rural Coverage of Banks (RCB_t)

After nationalization, the banks were diverted by the RBI to give priority to rural and non-banked areas in the bank branch expansion to enhance the credit availability to the needy. There is a continuous problem of mounting overdue. Poor quality of lending contributed to cumulative losses, adversely affecting the viability and efficiency of the banking system. After the initiation of reforms in the year 1991, banks were directed to close down loss making branches which are mainly functioned at rural areas or merge them with other existing banks. Thus closure of loss making banks together with the increasing population pressure may have reduced the credit flow to agriculture, and hence, the variable of RCB is expected to have a negative association with credit flow to agriculture.

3.4. Methodology to Estimate the Impact of the Macroeconomic Factors on Institutional Credit

Control of credit is considered as one of the important functions of central bank. Too much of or too little credit will have considerable effects on Indian economy. Determination of appropriate level of credit in an economy is crucial exercise. This has to be done in the context of the overall objectives of the macro economic and monetary policies of the government. There are varieties of instruments available to achieve this process. These are referred as instruments of credit control or weapons of credit control. The main intention of this study is to study the interlinkage between the credit supply (limited to agricultural sector) and macro economic variables. There is an argument that agriculture sector is insulated from macro level changes and several studies proved that it is not possible for agricultural sector. To attain the objective this study has developed a model by considering several theories. The interaction between institutional credit to agriculture and macroeconomic variables are disused here.

One of the prominent works of Stock and Watson (2001)[1] tells that Macro econometricians do four things: describe and summarize macroeconomic data, make macroeconomic forecasts, quantify what we do or do not know about the true structure of the macro economy, and advice (and sometimes become) macroeconomic policymakers. In the 1970s, these four tasks – data description, forecasting, structural inference, and policy analysis – were performed using a variety of techniques. Two basic groups of models are usually used for credit modeling. The first group of models tries to estimate the individual risk of the debtors. These are involved in credit risk assessment of commercial banks. These models are called individual credit risk models. Macroeconomic indicators can be part of these inputs for this type of models. In recent years a lot of papers, study the influence of the macroeconomic environment on the credit risk models. Some empirical macroeconomic models may formed in the literature. These models try to find the empirical observed relationship between the default rate and some macroeconomic indicators. This relationship is usually modeled with linear, probit or logit models. Static or dynamic approaches are applied for modeling. Vector Auto Regressive (VAR) models are one which are used in the case of dynamic model. These models are able to capture the mutual relationship of time series even in the case of time series which is non stationary in nature.

These ranged from large models with hundreds of equations, to single equation models that focused on interactions of a few variables to simple univariate time series models involving only a single variable. But after the macroeconomic chaos of the 1970s, none of these approaches appeared especially trustworthy. Christopher Sims (1980) provided a new macro econometric framework that held great promise: Vector Auto Regression (VAR). A univariate auto regression is a single-equation, single-variable linear model in which the current value of a variable is explained by its own lagged values. A VAR is a n-equation, n-variable linear model in

[1]Stock and Watson (2001), *"Vector Auto Regressions"*, http://faculty.washington.edu/ ezivot/econ584/stck_watson var.pdf

which each variable is in turn explained by its own lagged values, plus current and past values of the remaining n-1 variables. This simple framework provides a systematic way to capture rich dynamics in multiple time series, and the statistical toolkit that came with VARs was easy to use and interpret.

Brooks and Tsolacos (1999)[1] employ a VAR methodology for investigating the interaction between UK property market and various macro economic variables. The selection of the variables for the inclusion in the VAR model is governed by the time series that are commonly included in studies of credit predictability. It is assumed that credit supply are related to macro economic conditions and time series data is used here to gauge the current and future direction in the emerging economy like in India.

Bhide et al. 2005[2] argues that Economy-wide models, of macroeconomic variety or the CGE type, provide a comprehensive analytical structure for analysis. One limitation of the macroeconomic models is of course that much effort is needed to build the structural equations that incorporate the various inter-relationships and it is often difficult to check for the impact of changes in polices due to changes in the structure. A more flexible approach to the assessment of the impact of impulses emanating from the macroeconomic factors to agriculture is the framework of time series analysis. The VAR approach essentially captures the 'reduced form' relationships among the selected variables. Interpreting the estimated linkages in a theoretical framework is not easy because the theoretical specification is not complete in a VAR.

This chapter is an attempt to assess the nature of the interrelationship between selected macroeconomic factors and agriculture using the Vector Auto Regression (VAR) approach. The VAR approach provides a general framework for assessing the impact of inter-related variables. The general framework of analysis we adopt here is to specify a set of variables that capture the performance of agriculture and a set of variables that specify the macroeconomic environment. According to Sims Christopher[3] who awarded with Nobel in 2011 for this contribution, if there is true simultaneity among a set of variables, they should all be treated on an equal footing. There should not be any priori distinction between endogenous and exogenous variables. In simultaneous equation models, some variables are treated as endogenous and some as

---

[1]Brooks, and Tsolacos (1999), "The Impact of Economic and Financial Factors on UK Property Performance", *Journal of Property Research*, 16,2, Pp. 139-152.

[2]Bhide and Vani (2005), Op.Cit.

[3]*Sims Christopher* shared the Nobel Prize with *Thomas Sergent* for their contribution in Macro econometric framework in the year 2011.

exogenous or pre-determined (exogenous plus lagged endogenous). Before we estimate such models, we have to make sure that equations in the systems are identified. The identification is often achieved by assuming that some of the predetermined variables are present only in some equations. The decision is often subjective and has been surely criticized by Sims[1]. In this chapter the VAR model is employed as the variables used as a mix of aggregate and financial variables provide credit to agriculture in different forms. VAR performs well not only in capturing the data generating process of macroeconomic aggregates but also in capturing the contemporaneous and lagged relation between real economy and banking sector without imposing any apriori theorization.[2] The impact of the selected macroeconomic variables on the commercial bank credit flow to agriculture is measured through Vector Auto Regression Model with co-effiecients. The relevant shocks are identified by the Granger causality tests and the response of the system to these shocks is analyzed by the IRFs and Forecast Error Variance Decomposition (FEVD). Before explaining the detailed methodology, here the stationary properties of the time series data and the determination of the lag order of the VAR model are discussed.

3.5. Vector Auto Regression (VAR)

There are direct effects of changes in macroeconomic conditions on agriculture and these effects are further influenced by inter-relationships within agriculture. The macroeconomic variables themselves are inter-related and the impact of one change influences the others and the impact on agriculture is not limited to just the change in one factor. Hence, the Vector Auto Regressive method is a suitable econometric tool to analyse such inter-relationships.

The Vector Auto Regression (VAR) representation of variables allows an assessment of the inter-relationship in a dynamic framework. Although this representation has often been termed 'a-theoretic', choice of the variables in the VAR can be guided by theory.

This section presents a Vector Auto Regression (VAR) analysis. The VAR model assumes that the commercial banks credit to agriculture and macroeconomic variables can be described by the following structural form equation:

An unrestricted VAR model (Sims 1980) is written as follows:

$$Y_t = c + A(L) Y_t + e_t \quad \text{....................(1)}$$

[1]Gujarathi Damodar (2010), *"Basic Econommetrics"*, Mc Graw Hill Higher Education.

[2]Graeve, Thomas Kick and Michael Koetter (2008) , "Monetary Policy and Bank Distress: an Integrated Micro-macro Approach", *Deutsche Bundesbank Discussion Paper Series* 2, Banking and Financial Studies No.03/2008.

Here, Y_t is a vector containing each of the n variables included in the VAR

To model our empirical framework this if fitted as follows

$$AC_t = c + A\ (L)\ Y_t + B\ (L)\ ME_t + e_t$$

A(L) and B (L) is an (n´n) polynomial matrix of co-efficient in the back-shift operator L with lag length p,

$$\text{i.e., } A(L) = A_1\ L + A_2\ L_2 + \dots + Ap\ Lp\ ;$$

Y_t is a $n \times 1$ vector of endogenous agricultural credit variables; and ME_t is a $k \times 1$ vector of exogenous macroeconomic variables.

c is an (n´1) vector of intercept terms

e_t is an (n´1) vector of white noise error terms.

Stationary Tests of Endogenous Variables

The unique feature of time series analysis is to ensure that the taken variable ensures stationary. Augmented Dickey Fuller (ADF, 1979), Phillips-Perron(PP, 1988), Generalized Least Squares (GLS) de-trended Dickey-Fuller test (by Elliot, Rothenberg, and Stock, 1996) henceforth known as DF-GLS test and Kwiatkowski, Phillips, Schmidt & Shin (KPSS,1993) are widely used tests to check for the stationary of the variables.[1] This study has used ADF and PP unit root tests to ensure the stationary process.

Determination of Optimal Lag Length

The VAR model is used to estimate symmetric lags indicating the same lag length for all variables in all the equations of the model. Symmetric lag VAR model is easily estimated since the specification of all equations of the model are the same and estimation by OLS yields efficient estimates. On the issue of the lag-length selection, a maximum of 12 lags is considered and five criteria namely Likelihood Ratio (LR), Final Prediction Error (FPE), Akaike Information Criterion (AIC), Schwarz Information Criterion (SIC) and Hannan & Quinn Information Criterion (HQIC) are considered. The smallest value for each criterion corresponding to a certain lag length is chosen as the lag length for that criterion. The choice of appropriate lag order of the VAR model is based on these criteria and the diagnostic tests that test the presence of autocorrelation and heteroskadasticity in the residuals. AIC and HQIC criteria were used to determine the optimum lag length.[2]

---

[1]Brooks, and Tsolacos (1999), Op. Cit., Pp. 139-152.

[2]Ray (2008), Op.Cit.

Granger Causality Tests

Before getting on to estimate the impulse response functions and to carrying out the variance decomposition analysis, causality relationship between macroeconomic and agricultural performance variables was examined. The causality analysis is carried out within the framework of 'Block Causality' of variables in the VAR. The 'Granger Block Causality' tests allow an assessment of the strength of the transmission mechanisms (Bhide et al. 2005).[1] A variable x is said to *Granger cause* a variable y if past values of x are useful for predicting values of y. Rejection of H0 through the standard F-test attests to the inclusion of a particular variable in the inclusion of another variable.

Impulse Response Functions

The VAR framework permits us to examine the 'impulse response functions' of one of the variables in the VAR to shocks in the other variables. The stochastic error terms called impulses or innovations or shocks in the language of VAR. In other words, this study is able to assess the response of agricultural credit to macroeconomic shocks in a VAR framework. Bhide quoted that the results of VAR analysis would be sensitive to the ordering of variables in the VAR. For example, if we have a VAR of three variables, viz., y1, y2 and y3 then the results may vary if we specify VAR as (y1,y2, y3) or (y2, y1, y3) or (y3, y2, y1). To overcome the ambiguity, the 'generalised impulse response functions' have been developed by Pesaran and Shin in the year 1998.

3.6. Results and Interpretation

Table 3.1 signifies that the Variables included in the VAR model are required to be stationary in order to carry out joint significance tests on the lags of the variables. All the variables are subjected to Augmented Dickey Fuller (ADF) tests and P.P tests to observe unit root in the selected data. For the VAR analysis it is necessary to combine only the stationary variables. The results of the ADF and PP tests reveal that it is integrated in the order of one. These results suggest that this study should include first differences of the variables involved in framing the VAR model. While estimating the VAR, it is compulsory to specify the lag length of the variables to be included in the analysis. There are several criteria available to determine the lag length and the AIC criterion was used in determining the lag length of the VARs.

[1]Bhide and Vani (2005), Op.Cit.

From the Table 3.2 it is found that the existence of a statistical underlying relationship between macro characteristics and agricultural credit provides a basis for the assessment of the nature of the impact of macro level characteristics in supplying institutional credit towards agriculture. Granger block causality tests were used to find out the relationship between aggregate level and institutional credit to agriculture. Here, an attempt is made to capture the macro level characteristics of the economy and aggregate banking level indicators for institutional credit to agriculture by using several variables as mentioned in Table 3.2.

Table 3.1: Stationary Statistics over the Selected Variables

	Augmented Dickey-Fuller (ADF)			**Phillip-Perron (PP)**		
Var.+	**Level**	**First Difference**	**Con.**	**Level**	**First Difference**	**Con.**
ADL	-0.932 (0.766)	-4.790* (0.000)	I (1)	-0.865 (0.788)	-4.781* (0.000)	I (1)
AGDP	-0.401 (0.898)	-5.768* (0.000)	I (1)	-0.403 (0.898)	-5.763* (0.000)	I (1)
CRR	-1.715 (0.415)	-7.886* (0.000)	I (1)	-1.677 (0.434)	-7.823* (0.000)	I (1)
CRRBL	-0.968 (0.754)	-3.774* (0.006)	I (1)	-0.883 (0.782)	-3.899* (0.004)	I (1)
DFA	-1.511 (0.517)	-3.654* (0.009)	I (1)	-1.634 (0.455)	-3.855* (0.005)	I (1)
IDA	0.516 (0.985)	-3.777* (0.006)	I (1)	0.740 (0.991)	-3.849* (0.005)	I (1)
WPI	-1.412 (0.566)	-5.293* (0.000)	I (1)	-1.412 (0.566)	-5.266* (0.000)	I (1)
INVSL	-0.762 (0.818)	-6.758* (0.000)	I (1)	-1.120 (0.697)	-7.099* (0.000)	I (1)
RCB	-0.891 (0.780)	-3.009** (0.043)	I (1)	-1.339 (0.601)	-2.977** (0.046)	I (1)
TFA	-0.999 (0.743)	-3.842* (0.005)	I (1)	-0.991 (0.746)	-3.965* (0.004)	I (1)

Note: * and ** denote rejection of a unit root hypothesis based on Mckinnon critical values at 1% and 5% respectively. +Description of the variables: ADL: Natural log of Aggregate Deposits, AGDP: Gross Capital formation in Agriculture divided by share of GDP in agriculture; CRR: Cash Reserve Ratio; CRRBL: Credit Provided by Co-operatives and Regional Rural Banks; DFA: Direct Finance to Agriculture; IDA: Indirect Finance to Agriculture; WPI: Whole Sale Price Index; INVSL: Investment in Statutory Securities; RCB: Ratio of Rural branches to Total Branches; TFA: Total Finance to Agriculture.

Table 3.2: Block Causality over the Selected Variables

Block Causality from (Selected Macro Variables)	Causality to	Test statistic
(ADL, AGDP,CRR,CRRBL, WPI, INVSL,RCB)	DFA	53.83*(0.000)
(ADL, AGDP,CRRBL, WPI, INVSL,RCB)	DFA	58.51*(0.000)
(ADL, AGDP,CRR,CRRBL, WPI, INVSL,RCB)	IDF	18.96(0.166)
(ADL, AGDP,CRR,CRRBL, WPI, INVSL)	IDF	20.48(0.058)
(ADL, AGDP,CRR,CRRBL, WPI, INVSL,RCB)	TFAL	49.98*(0.000)

Note: Data used for the period 1970-71 to 2010-11; Order of VAR=2; Test statistic is based on the log likelihood ratio test of the null hypothesis of no causality.

* Significance Level at 1 percentage.

This table presents the results of block causality tests on three different institutional credit variables and selected set of macro level characteristics. It is observed that the evidence of block causality from macro level characteristics to direct agricultural credit shows strong relationship. This is even more acute, when we omit CRR from the group. Here, the null hypothesis which carries no relationship between macro characteristics to DFA is rejected at one percentage level of significance. The block causality from the macro level variables to IDF appears as insignificant when we included the whole group of variables. By analysing the individual granger cause the RCB is omitted and there is a significant relationship with this subset.

Table 3.3: Impulse Response of Direct Finance to Agriculture over the Selected Variables

Item	Year 1	Year 2	Year 3	Cumulative Impact		
				5 Years	10 Years	25 Years
7-MVAR+						
ADL	0.693523	0.788091	3.712469	6.186359	15.04931	17.74526
AGDPL	0.391078	0.209997	-0.14742	-0.410838	-1.937144	2.955291
CRR	0.424481	0.550482	-0.27439	-1.635349	-1.730114	-6.361641
CRRBL	0.163928	0.657543	1.325516	2.301741	10.70673	3.825473
WPI	1.369093	3.607730	12.29356	20.28227	48.66208	23.03949
INVSL	-0.12864	-0.19331	-2.25171	-3.897541	-9.762570	-5.477718
RCB	0.273467	0.555374	1.583580	3.576304	16.88777	4.090380
5-MVAR+						
ADL	0.363268	0.293536	0.610950	0.852426	2.778423	15.86651
CRR	0.249725	0.791139	0.894395	0.987831	-0.2519	-18.0981
CRRBL	0.269593	0.827637	1.445224	2.375173	8.485787	3.530666
WPI	0.719308	3.057757	5.688861	8.258354	13.21708	7.844583
RCB	-0.00451	-0.22032	0.175301	1.465570	20.67923	5.118136
3-MVAR+						
CRRBL	0.766261	1.262653	1.088912	0.120117	7.736662	-4.235331
INVSL	1.760698	9.815772	15.09141	24.65275	67.23700	42.93367
RCB	1.484023	3.290307	4.832287	10.55664	46.89704	10.94457
2-MVAR+						
CRRBL	0.291317	1.114583	2.448566	6.304380	19.51544	63.48835
RCB	0.353276	0.939656	1.538892	2.150979	-2.568430	-60.92320

In Table 3.3 the Impulse response functions to the DFA are summarized for the impact from one year to three years and impact for 5,10,25 years. The positive impact of rise in ADL throughout the period suggests that the agriculture sector benefits from the saving habit of the masses. The positive impact of AGDPL is for initial two years and up to 10 years. It shows negative impact which shows that capital formation may not act as substitute by direct finance to agriculture. The reason behind this is that government is reluctant in giving importance to agriculture as compared to industry. Even the minimum supportive price announced by the government, sometimes may not cover the input made by the farmers. The influence of middlemen, monsoon failure, seasonal nature of the product, poor storage facilities are factors which limit the share of agriculture in GDP. The study observed that the increase in CRR shows initially the positive response with the direct credit to agriculture but after 2 years it is consistently negative in providing credit towards agriculture. Initially, Co-operative and regional rural banks take a lead in providing agricultural credit and only in later stage there is increasing share of DFA by commercial banks and shift has moved from co-operative to commercial banking in catering the needs of the agricultural sector. Investment in statutory securities is one of the methods of the government in restraining credit supply. But even at the point of view of the banker, it is safer to invest in government securities.

RCB variable shows the number of rural branches to total bank branches in India. When, the higher the number of rural branches results in increasing the outlay on direct finance to agriculture. 5M-VAR, 3M-VAR, and 2M-VAR including direct finance to agriculture confirms the pattern of impulse seen in 7M-VAR. The reductions in different VAR frameworks are used to get noticeable changes in the framework.

Table 3.4: Impulse Response of Indirect Finance to Agriculture over the Selected Variables

Item	Year 1	Year 2	Year 3	Cumulative Impact		
				5 Years	10 Years	25 Years
7-MVAR+						
ADL	0.223648	4.330565	11.13525	15.46928	7.167809	-9.360302
AGDPL	-0.956426	-1.005824	-1.003282	-0.908394	2.919172	9.236696
CRR	-0.982001	-2.121946	-2.595920	-2.821115	-9.714084	-33.86790
CRRBL	-1.295671	-2.175598	-2.928376	-4.047416	-6.637356	-4.277187
WPI	-3.832452	1.703576	15.52582	20.83196	1.930953	-30.07033
INVSL	-0.155741	-2.958360	-7.521799	-9.078949	-1.835845	16.42936
RCB	-0.372354	-0.449171	1.682566	4.530751	-23.43302	-94.97447
5-MVAR+						
ADL	-0.468422	0.154132	0.937525	3.453915	7.385811	6.569017
CRR	-0.912408	-1.020327	-2.564895	-3.147560	-14.90043	-49.66634
CRRBL	-0.951060	-1.346877	-1.829963	-2.194983	-5.569347	-6.259474
INVSL	-0.525976	-0.901092	-1.365632	-1.699230	-1.707725	4.749240
RCB	1.033822	3.271900	7.764777	10.76255	-19.01308	-112.5037
3-MVAR+						
CRRBL	-0.391952	-0.262090	0.413121	1.029496	5.799022	4.665036
INVSL	-0.162301	0.044498	0.343820	1.833111	6.155963	18.96485
RCB	0.924793	2.037223	3.101948	-1.017586	-36.39534	-124.2089
2-MVAR+						
CRRBL	-0.361307	-0.767746	-1.189303	-1.481107	1.495935	13.80060
RCB	-1.095004	-2.572969	-5.475433	-16.19262	-67.04834	-238.8366

In table 3.4 the Impulse response functions to the IDF are summarised for the impact from the one year to 3 years and impact for 5,10,25 years. The positive impact of rise in ADL throughout the period suggests that the agriculture sector benefits from the saving habit of the masses. The above result clearly tells about the positive shock of aggregate level deposits to indirect finance to agriculture. The negative impact of AGDPL is for initial three years which reveals that there is lack of effect in that short term period. There is a positive impact of indirect credit flow to agriculture on the tenth year onwards shows that the growth always fuels the credit delivery and vice versa. It is observed that the impulses are uniformly negative for the CRR throughout the period. CRR is considered as one of the important policy channels of the central bank in India. It clearly indicated that there is an immediate and consistent long term negative relationship between CRR and indirect finance to agriculture. The general hypothesis is that Higher the credit provided by CRRBL (Co-operative and Regional Rural Banks) shows lower the commercial bank credit because Co-operative societies and Regional Rural Banks are considered as one of the substituted institutional frameworks to focus on agriculture alone. Perhaps, if there is an increasing trend in the share of IDF by commercial banks there will be a decreasing trend in the flow of credit towards agriculture. This result is not consistent with all the VAR frameworks. Some of the reduced frameworks show positive result too.

Investments in statutory securities are more safe and secured. Banks may prefer to invest more in securities rather than in agriculture credit. This may restrict the credit supply in other ways and mitigate the risk in lending process. RCB means shows the number of rural branches to total bank branches in India. There is a quiet interesting negative relationship between rural branches and indirect finance to agriculture. The nature of the indirect finance to agriculture is different from the direct finance to agriculture. IDF is mainly to facilitate on agriculture equipments and so on. IDF is mainly urban focused. 5M-VAR, 3M-VAR, and 2M-VAR including indirect finance to agriculture confirms the pattern of impulse seen in 7M-VAR.

Table 3.5: Impulse Response of Total Finance to Agriculture over the Selected Variables

Item	Year1	Year 2	Year 3	Cumulative Impact		
				5 Years	10 Years	25 Years
7-MVAR+						
ADL	0.280139	0.403090	1.970498	6.070417	12.56972	10.50648
AGDPL	0.197246	-0.130330	-0.440690	-1.193616	-2.285040	5.039588
CRR	0.448054	0.478314	-0.087407	-1.757435	-2.326986	-1.885525
CRRBL	1.023464	1.779240	2.825743	6.663544	23.45655	-2.733597
WPI	-0.599753	0.886983	8.672137	22.02023	37.34577	1.700634
INVSL	0.264976	0.169394	-1.675966	-4.451211	-8.780444	-0.512500
RCB	0.601109	0.375026	0.060254	0.537557	16.79553	6.564315
5-MVAR+						
ADL	-0.302657	-1.236476	-2.097527	-2.866321	-0.262737	13.70557
CRR	0.041416	0.215477	0.271288	-0.319494	-4.357505	-22.52919
CRRBL	1.159583	1.795196	2.918656	6.379794	18.34308	-0.689767
WPI	0.191735	0.879183	1.627847	2.918178	3.651899	1.411446
RCB	0.285170	0.210537	0.504722	2.676050	19.12056	-12.74408
3-MVAR+						
CRRBL	0.936013	2.433652	4.492186	9.576644	21.09990	11.91872
INVSL	-0.181805	-0.335842	-0.478678	-0.535567	1.316559	12.26433
RCB	0.903340	2.027916	3.391043	6.437962	13.09594	-10.35693
2-MVAR+						
CRRBL	1.032215	3.093388	6.162338	14.90779	46.96090	154.9206
RCB	0.177237	0.007173	-0.586671	-2.955200	-12.20057	-22.40829

In Table 3.5 the Impulse response functions to the TFA are summarized to study the impact from one year to 3 years and impact for 5,10,25 years. The positive impact of rise in ADL throughout the period suggests that the agriculture sector benefits from the saving habit of the masses. Here, one can notice the positive shock of aggregate level deposits to total finance to agriculture. This also proves that excess deposits channeled through different productive sectors includes social sector also.

The negative impact of AGDPL is for initial ten years, which reveals that there is lack of effect in short term period. There is a positive impact of indirect credit flow to agriculture on the twenty fifth years onwards. It shows the capital formation in the name of credit. It is interpreted that the impulses are showing mixed results for the CRR throughout the period. CRR is considered as one of the important policy channels of the central bank in India. It is possible that there is lack of immediate effect of increasing of cash reserves in the flow of finance to agriculture.

Co-operative societies and Regional Rural Banks are considered as one of the substituted institutional frameworks which focus mainly on agriculture. The relationship between total finance to agriculture and credit given by co-operatives and regional rural banks show consistent positive impact. This may be due to the governments overall objective to enhance the flow of credit to agriculture sector. It shows negative effect in the long term period. Investment in government securities shows positive for two years but is consistently negative for the whole period. It clearly tells that policy variables always negative to the credit flow to agriculture. It is observed that the rural branch totally encourages the total finance to the agriculture sector. This result is consistent with the different VAR frameworks.

3.7. Conclusion

In this chapter an attempt was made to examine the effect of macroeconomic variables on the changes in the institutional credit flow to agriculture in an emerging country like India. By considering the importance of agriculture sector, this study documents the impact of macroeconomic variables on institutional credit level. The VAR procedure was employed to study the interrelationship between variables. This empirical work confirms that the responses of institutional credit to macroeconomic variables are considerable and it proves that agriculture sector is not insulated. The reductions in different VAR frameworks are used to get noticeable changes in the framework. 7M-VAR, 5M-VAR, 3M-VAR, and 2M-VAR including institutional finance to agriculture confirm the mixed pattern of impulse responses.

CHAPTER IV

BANK LEVEL VARIABLES AND AGRICULTURAL CREDIT BY COMMERCIAL BANKS

4.1. Introduction

The initialisation of the Banking sector reforms in the 90s is considered as the process of economic liberalisation adopted by India which encourages the arrival of foreign banks in the banking sector. With the presence of foreign banks in the Indian market, the banks in Indian market have to face tough competition. There is a need for Indian banks to recover from their sloth and to be vibrant. Banking is an important sector which acts as a backbone of economic progress. The credit markets in India functioned normally even during the turbulent times in contrast to the intense credit freeze experienced by some of the advanced economies. However, there was a general decline in demand for credit due to the economic slowdown set in by the spillover effects of global financial turmoil. In response to the financial turmoil, the Reserve Bank initiated several measures mainly to impart liquidity in the banking system and to channelize the credit to crisis affected sectors.[1]

The banks render vital services to the masses belonging to the various sectors of the economy like agriculture, industry whether small scale or large scale. The banking system is one of the few institutions that impinges on the economy which affects its performance for better or worse. Banks act as development agencies and are the sources of hope and aspirations of the masses.[2] The persistence of global recession is providing a testing time for the financial sector in general and banking sector in particular all over the world. Handling the spill-over effects of the financial turmoil has turned out to be more challenging for the Governments and Central Bank as the impact of the crisis has become wider and deeper. The unsettling conditions in the global financial markets warranted institution of swift and appropriate policy measures. While the Governments all over the world continue to pursue expansionary fiscal policies, central banks took several measures (conventional and non-conventional) to ease liquidity, stimulate demand and moderate the impact of the global downturn and credit crunch on their economies. The crisis once again brought to the fore the issue of financial stability and, thus, triggered a discussion on counter-cyclical fiscal, monetary and prudential measures.[3]

---

[1]Report of RBI, (2009), Recent Trend and Progress of Banking in India.

[2]Sooden, Meenakshi (1992), *"Regional Disparities of Commercial Banking in India"*, Delhi: Kanishka Publishing House.

[3]Report of RBI, (2009) Recent Trend and Progress of Banking in India.

Banking is an important segment of the teritory sector and acts as a backbone of economic progress. Banking sector is undergoing fundamental changes that have diluted its traditional role of protecting small deposits against capital and income risk and facilitating the conversion of savings into investment. The banking leaders have identifies these issues and opportunities and have started to design their global financial strategy accordingly.

As an economic institution, banks are supposed to be more directly and positively related to the performance of the economy than most non economic institutions are. Schumpeter, the first modern economist, regarded the banking system as one of the two key agents in the whole process of economic development. The role of commercial banks occupied a new meaning and significance, in view of the changing structure and requirements of a developing economy. The increased horizon of commercial banks identifies itself with the problems and responsibilities for making banking an instrument for bringing about social and economic transformation of developing country. Social responsibilities have undergone far reaching changes. Banks have become the prime movers and pace setters for the achievement of socio economic objectives of the country.[1]

4.2. Changing Role of Commercial Banks

The commercial banks provide a range of services to the whole community in many ways. Apart from the basic banking services such as deposits, loans and advances, banks have been traditionally rendering certain ancillary services also to their customers. Among the services introduced by modern commercial banks during the last quarter of century, the credit cards deserve special mention. By providing these diversified services, banks help in the growth of trade and industry to a great extent[2]. The present financial system in India is large with a variety of banks, financial institutions, capital market institutions, non-banking institution and a number of indigenous banks. Among the financial institutions in India, banks are prominent financial intermediaries and in fact, financial inter-mediation is largely synonymous with banking[3].

Banking operations in India are controlled by the Reserve Bank of India. Broadly, the Indian financial system can be divided into organised and unorganised segments. The organised sector consists of banking institutions and non-banking institutions. Banking institutions are

---

[1]Dholkia, Vakul. H. (1996), *"Total Factor Productivity in Indian Agriculture"*, National Seminar on Agricultural Development Perspective for the IX Five Year Plan, 13-15 June.

[2]Shekar, K.C. (1974), *"Banking Theory and Practice"*, Sahibabad: Bikas Publishing House Pvt. Ltd., Pp. 7-9.

[3]Ajit,D.(1997), "The Role of Banks in Economic Development of India", *Prajnan*, 25 .

further divided into development banks, co-operative banks and commercial banks. Unorganised financial market operations consist of hundis, money lending, chit funds etc.[1]

Commercial banks play an important role in mobilizing savings of economically surplus units, which are widely scattered. Commercial banks, in view of their vast branch network spread over the country, obtaining the savings on a short or medium term basis, are places in an especially privileged position to collect them. If the banks fail to tap these savings, the surplus money lying idle in the hands of the people could not be of any use in nation's endeavor of economic development. Savings and investments are the most important ingredients of capital formation for an economy. The promotion of domestic savings is must to boost the process of capital formation and development. In fact capital formation is a function of generation, mobilization and canalization of savings in to productive activities; the commercial banks are in the nature of a catalyst, converting savings in to capital for productive investment.

When the savings of economically surplus units are pooled together in commercial banks, it results in a large reservoir of social capital. It helps in capital formation and capital accumulation which are very necessary for building infrastructure and setting up of basic and key industries. Among the factors determining economic growth in under developed countries, capital is of supreme importance. Developing economies do not suffer as much from a lack of national resources as they do from under utilization of the existing resources. Capital formation largely depends on the effectiveness of institutions, which funnel the capital flows. While increasing rate of capital formation it is very important to build an efficient commercial banking system equipped with an adequate coverage so that apart from mobilizing savings, it may also be able to foster the banking habits in a society.

Lewis has emphasised the key role of bank credit in bringing about a structural transformation of an underdeveloped economy. In the expansion of the capitalist sector, bank credit becomes a factor of fundamental importance. Keynes and Schumpeter too have emphasized the role of credit in economic development. It is important that the hindrances and rigidities, which operate in the underdeveloped economies, should not be strengthened by paucity of credit. David Rockfeller, chairman of Manhattan Bank pointed out that the innovator looked to the bank for credit he needed to carry out his plans. Ultimately it was the banker who provided the basic fuel credit for economic growth.

---

[1]ibid., p. 38.

4.3. Overall Trend and Progress & Genesis of Banking Business in India

Banking in India is as old as ancient Vedic period. However the English agency house established the first modern bank known as the Bank of Hindustan at Calcutta in 1770. After that Bengal Bank was setup in 1784 and around 1786 General bank of India was established, but these banks could not provide the services due to their own crises. The major banking events during the inter war period were the amalgamation of the three Presidency Banks into the Imperial Bank of India in 1921 and the setting up of the Reserve Bank of India in 1935. Though Imperial Bank of India was a commercial entity, it performed the governments functions and acted as an agent of the then government. It acted as bankers' bank and was the sole note issuing authority. It also managed the government debt and also maintained the government balances. The State Bank of India was established in 1935 and acted as a banker's bank and an agent of the government.

Under the forces of liberalisation and globalisation, many banking institutions have expanded beyond their home countries and traditional lines of business leading to emergence of large international banks. Many product innovations and new ways of doing business have also emerged that have led to widespread use of securitisation, derivatives and other financial products linking traditional banking functions to the operations of capital markets, whereas these developments have led to some degree of efficiency in financial intermediation, new issues have emerged over the past year that merit attention. Most, if not all of these large banks have become financial conglomerates operating in all the different segments of the financial sector. This movement has been enabled both by technological developments leading to faster transmission of financial transactions and financial innovations, and by falling national barriers allowing cross border capital flows.[1]

Though, they operate in the rural areas, yet unorganized money market activities are quite significant in the urban areas also. There is no precise estimate of the size of the unorganized money market in India. It is generally expected that the relative size of the unorganized money market transactions would decline over time.

The forces of deregulation, technology and globalisation have increased competitive pressures, which have (a) Unleashed the strong forces of restructuring and consolidation with the number of banks declining all over the world, (b) Prompted banks to seek new sources of revenue beyond traditional products. These, in turn, have led to the blurring of distinctions among providers of various financial services and emergence of financial conglomerates.

---

[1]Report of RBI (2009), Report on Currency and Finance in India.

4.3.1. *Branch Expansion*

Rapid economic development pre-supposes rapid expansion of commercial banks. Initially, the banks were conservative and opened branches mainly in metropolitan cities and other major cities. Branch expansion gained momentum after nationalisation of major commercial banks and the introduction of the Lead Bank Scheme. The number of bank offices of Scheduled Commercial Banks in India registered comparatively a higher rate of increase i.e. 332 percentage in the post-nationalisation period.[1]

Table 4.1: Sectorwise Branch Expansion during 2007 to 2011

Category/ Year	**SBI & Associates**	**Nationalised Banks**	**Public Sector Banks**	**Old Private Sector Banks**	**New Private Sector Banks**	**Foreign Banks**
2007	14130	35858	50168	4819	2016	259
2008	14673	37431	52104	4826	2598	272
2009	15846	39234	55080	4690	3632	279
2010	16878	40854	57732	4908	4328	295
2011	18114	43187	61301	5174	5213	310
CGAR %	15.791	11.15	12.28	3.72	74.19	10.67
Mean	15928.20	39312.80	55277.00	4883.40	3557.40	283.00
S.D.	1619.85	2866.52	4430.69	180.21	1288.10	19.91
C.V.	10.17	7.29	8.02	3.69	36.21	7.04
Skew.	0.34	0.25	0.33	1.20	0.09	0.33

Source: Statistical Tables Related to Banks in India Various Issues, RBI Publication.

From the above table, it is found that the total number of branches in India was increased in all sectors of Banks. The number of branches of SBI has increased from 14,130 to 18,114. The number of branches of nationalised banks has increased from 35,858 to 43,187. The same trend continues in public sector, private sector and foreign banks also. It is observed that the private sector banks have a phenomenal growth compared to this sectors. It is also observed that all the sectors in the sample are positively skewed. With increasing number of bank branches, the average population per bank branch has improved from 15,583 in 2001 to 12,601 in 2012. With liberalization of the branch licensing policy and drive towards financial inclusion, the share of rural and semi urban branches in total new branches opened reached 69.8 percentage during 2011-12.

[1]Majumdar, (2005), "Risk Philosophy: An Enquiry into Risks and Uncertainties in Agriculture and the Role of Credit", *Occasional Paper No.41, Dept. Of Economic Analysis and Research,* NABARD, Mumbai.

4.3.2. *Employees Expansion*

In a service industry like banking, it is not possible to measure physical output in the absence of clear definition. However, most of the measures that are used to study banks' performance can be interpreted more correctly by measuring the banks efficiency target rather than directly measuring their productivity. The level of efficiency of banks is commonly measured at the level of employees, which is the important wheel on which banking industry moves.

Table 4.2: Sectorwise Employees Expansion during 2007 to 2011

Category/ Year	SBI & Associates	Nationalised Banks	Public Sector Banks	Old Private Sector Banks	New Private Sector Banks	Foreign Banks
2007	270608	473725	744333	51138	59367	22117
2008	255699	473179	728878	48667	88617	28426
2009	242029	466400	708429	48700	110123	33969
2010	268598	462926	731524	51341	124998	29582
2011	267332	467262	734594	54860	107424	27742
CGAR %	0.57	-1.13	-0.52	4.56	53.86	12.02
Mean	260853.20	468698.40	729551.60	50941.20	102105.80	28367.20
S.D.	12021.12	4637.05	13175.96	2537.25	28451.24	4251.92
C.V.	4.61	0.99	1.81	4.98	27.86	14.99
Skew.	-1.23	0.04	-1.10	0.95	-0.94	-0.36

Source: Statistical Tables Related to Banks in India Various Issues, RBI Publication.

The Table 4.2 discloses that the number of employees in all the sectors of banks has shown an increasing trend but higher growth level is posted by new private sector banks. There is a negative growth in the nationalised banks and overall public sector as well. This clearly depicts the new manpower pushed to the private sector bank due to increasing opportunities. New private sector banks shows 27.86 percentage as variation level during the study period. In case of SBI, Nationalised and Private Sector Banks the employee expansion has decreased gradually due to automation and mechanisation.

4.3.3. *Business Per Employee*

The average business per employee is an improved measure of efficiency of employee because the total business combines both deposits and advances. The intermediation process between savers and borrowers becomes complete when deposits mobilised are lent to borrowers engaged in different types of business activities. Business per employee is defined as the Aggregate Deposits plus Total Advances Divided by Total Numbers. of Employees.

Employee productivity in terms of both business per employee and profit per employee in all SCBs at aggregate level increased continuously in all the financial years during the period 2007-08 to 2011-12.

Table 4.3: Sectorwise Business Per Employee during 2007 to 2011

(Rs in Lakhs)

Category/ Year	SBI & Associates	Nationalised Banks	Public Sector Banks	Old Private Sector Banks	New Private Sector Banks	Foreign Banks
2007	337.79	383.07	366.61	417.33	889.39	955.41
2008	436.35	490.01	471.18	474.93	830.09	974.77
2009	565.06	618.28	600.10	569.32	831.96	1037.10
2010	650.22	783.16	734.35	638.43	787.15	1282.74
2011	735.52	947.40	870.29	700.02	840.71	1445.87
CGAR %	56.86	69.04	64.92	35.84	-3.74	28.92
Mean	544.99	644.38	608.51	560.01	835.86	1139.18
S.D.	160.09	225.76	201.13	115.58	36.44	215.58
C.V.	29.37	35.04	33.05	20.64	4.36	18.92
Skew.	-0.21	0.32	0.16	-0.08	0.32	0.84

Source: Statistical Tables Related to Banks in India Various Issues, RBI Publication.

From the table 4.3, it is observed that the sectorwise business per employee showed a mixed growth trend. In SBI & Associates, it has increased from 337.79 to 735.52; in the case of Nationalised Banks its has increased from 383.07 to 947.40; in the case of Public sector banks it has increased from 366.61 to 870.29; it reached to 840.71 from 889.39 in old private sector banks where it posts negative trend and it reached to 1445.87 in foreign banks from 955.41 over a period of five years. Table 4.3 reveals that the nationalised banks have given maximum variation when compared to other sectors. The total new private sector banks have shown negative growth during the study period. The table also indicates that all the sectors in the sample are positively skewed except old private sector banks.

4.3.4. Profit Per Employee

Profitability of banks facilitates many aspects, which includes, *inter alia*, enhancing the ability of banks to mobilise resources from the capital market, as well as better management of nonperforming assets. In addition, sound profitability of banks enhances their ability to augment the financial inclusion process. During the pre-liberalisation period, banks in India were operating in a rather tight regulatory environment. After liberalisation, Indian banks operated in a less regulated environment in terms of interest rate, liberalisation, reduction in reserve requirements, and entry deregulation. In addition, with the advent of complex financial products, banks' business has expanded in recent years beyond the traditional financial intermediation process.

Table 4.4: Sectorwise Profit per Employee during 2007 to 2011

(Rs in Lakhs)

Category/ Year	SBI & Associates	Nationalised Banks	Public Sector Banks	Old Private Sector Banks	New Private Sector Banks	Foreign Banks
2007	2.20	2.23	2.22	1.69	6.92	13.87
2008	2.57	2.87	2.76	2.31	6.03	16.13
2009	3.72	3.77	3.75	4.06	6.85	19.47
2010	4.43	4.86	4.70	4.69	6.77	25.39
2011	4.65	5.74	5.34	4.22	8.47	17.09
CGAR %	60	74.48	69.34	79.4	12.71	22.21
Mean	3.51	3.89	3.75	3.39	7.01	18.39
S.D.	1.09	1.43	1.30	1.31	0.89	4.40
C.V.	31.14	36.71	34.61	38.65	12.73	23.92
Skew.	-0.28	0.22	0.05	-0.59	1.27	1.17

Source: Statistical Tables Related to Banks in India Various Issues, RBI Publication.

From the table 4.4, it is interpreted that the sectorwise profit per employee shows positive trend for all the sectors concerned. In all categories of bank, the profit per employee was continuously increasing over the period of five years. More or Less it was doubled in all sectors. The old generation private sector banks have registered a big variation compared to other sectors. However, all the sectors have showed a positive growth during the study period. The table also shows that all the sectors in the sample are positively skewed except old private sector banks and SBI and its associates. In recent years, significant variation in profitability has been observed among bank groups. It was observed that, generally profitability of foreign banks was higher than that of other bank groups.

4.3.5. Capital Reserves & Surplus

The RBI released draft guidelines for implementing Basel III. As per the proposal, banks will have to augment the minimum core capital after a stringent deduction. The two new requirements – capital conservative buffer (an extra buffer of 2.5% to reduce risk) and a counter cyclical buffer (an extra capital buffer if possible during good times) – have also been introduced for banks.

Table 4.5: Sectorwise Capital Reserves & Surplus during 2007 to 2011

(Rs in Crore)

Category/ Year	SBI & Associates	Nationalised Banks	Public Sector Banks	Old Private Sector Banks	New Private Sector Banks	Foreign Banks
2007	37660	77384	115044	20171	34140	20171
2008	42941	92689	135630	10736	39736	33075
2009	61706	113079	174785	15315	76056	49332
2010	72422	135920	208342	17477	82192	59937
2011	83726	157276	241001	20171	99813	69061
CGAR %	62.95	51.4	55.17	56.84	93.75	85.45
Mean	59691.00	115269.60	174960.40	14676.60	66387.40	47143.80
S.D.	19427.73	32175.21	51508.68	4441.08	28331.65	18492.90
C.V.	32.55	27.91	29.44	30.26	42.68	39.23
Skew.	0.03	0.21	0.15	0.01	-0.19	-0.14

Source: Statistical Tables Related to Banks in India Various Issues, RBI Publication.

From the Table 4.5 it is clear that the sectorwise Capital Reserves & Surplus portrays positive trend for all the sectors during the study period. As for as the Capital Reserves & Surplus is concerned, all the sectors have shown positive growth during the study period. The Capital Reserves & Surplus of SBI has increased from 37,660 to 83,726 crores. In Nationalised banks it has increased from 77,384 to 1, 57,276 crores; Public Sector banks from 1, 15,044 to 2, 41,000 crores; Private Sector banks from 20171 to 69061 crores. Among these, the New Private Sector banks have registered a big variation than the other sector banks. The table also reveals that excepting Private Sector banks and Foreign banks, all the sectors are positively skewed.

4.3.6. Growth of Deposits

Savings and investments are the most important ingredients of capital formation for an economy. Therefore, the promotion of domestic savings is must to boost the process of capital formation and development. Thus, the commercial banks are in the nature of a catalyst, converting savings into capital for productive investment[1].

[1]Dhawan, (1975), "Role of Banks a Vehicle of Economic Progress and Instrument of Social Change", *The Banker*, December, p.25.

Table 4.6: Sectorwise Deposits during 2007 to 2011

(Rs in Crore)

Category/ Year	SBI & Associates	Nationalised Banks	Public Sector Banks	Old Private Sector Banks	New Private Sector Banks	Foreign Banks
2007	542409	1080072	1622481	130456	298000	237853
2008	633476	1360724	1994200	138249	413738	150750
2009	773875	1679993	2453868	165589	509444	191161
2010	1007041	2105706	3112747	199274	537104	214076
2011	542409	1080072	3691802	229897	592904	237853
CGAR %	54.6	65.23	61.79	41.21	45.77	52.26
Mean	812977.40	1762042.20	2575019.60	172693.00	470238.00	181517.00
S.D.	240679.65	597102.24	836019.23	41832.01	116096.19	49665.11
C.V.	29.60	33.89	32.47	24.22	24.69	27.36
Skew.	0.22	0.42	0.35	0.51	-0.82	-0.43

Source: Statistical Tables Related to Banks in India Various Issues, RBI Publication.

All the sectors of banks have shown positive growth during the study period. From the table 4.6, it is clear that the sectorwise deposits represents positive trend for all the sectors over the study period. The total deposits of SBI have increased from 5,42,409 to 5,42,409, Nationalised Banks from 10,80,072 to 10,80,072 crores. Public sector banks from 16,22,481 to 36,918,021 crores. The total deposit reached to 2,29,897 from 1,30,456 crores in old private sector banks and it reached to 2,37,853 crores in foreign banks from 2,37,853 over a period of five years. Table 4.6 reveals that the Nationalised banks have shown maximum variation when compared to other sectors. The table also shows that the all the sectors in the sample are positively skewed except new private sector banks and foreign banks.

4.3.7. *Growth in Investments*

The public sector banks have also been investing in shares, debentures and bonds of government and quasai- government bodies. Over a period of time, the proportion of this investment out of the total deposits had considerably gone up.

Table 4.7: Sectorwise Investments during 2007 to 2011

(Rs in Crore)

Category/ Year	SBI & Associates	Nationalised Banks	Public Sector Banks	Old Private Sector Banks	New Private Sector Banks	Foreign Banks
2007	224761	408796	633557	45254	135314	52384
2008	211875	452981	664856	43647	171008	71471
2009	263823	536018	799841	54080	224498	98910
2010	357624	655042	1012666	72393	234139	130354
2011	377658	828125	1205783	83499	270618	159286
CGAR %	43.26	50.68	48.17	48.97	47.92	91.65
Mean	287148.20	576192.40	863340.60	59774.60	207115.40	102481.00
S.D.	76258.02	169192.11	242792.97	17503.19	53675.40	43266.02
C.V.	26.56	29.36	28.12	29.28	25.92	42.22
Skew.	0.38	0.85	0.68	0.62	-0.37	0.25

Source: Statistical Tables Related to Banks in India Various Issues, RBI Publication.

From the table 4.7, it is observed that the sectorwise investments discloses positive trend for all the sectors over the study period. In SBI & Associates, it has increased from 2,24,761 to 3,77,658 crores, Nationalised banks from 4,08,796 to 8,28,125 crores. Public sector banks from 6,33,557 to 12,05,783 crores. The investment in old private sector banks has increased from 45,254 to 83,490 crores and foreign banks from 52,384 to 1,59,286 crores. Table 4.7 also reveals that the foreign banks have shown maximum variation when compared to other sector. Here, all the sectors of banks have shown positive growth during the study period. The table also shows that the all the sectors in the sample are positively skewed except new private sector banks.

4.3.8. Growth of Advances

Lending of funds to the constituents, mainly traders, business and industrial enterprises, constitutes the main business of the banking company. The major portion of a bank's funds is employed by way of loans and advances, which is the most profitable employment of its funds. The major part of banks' income is earned from interest and discount on the funds so advanced. Marketing in banking refers to buying and selling of money. In other words, to buy, it must promote marketing activities towards deposits and to sell them in the form of loans and advances. Banks are granting loans and advances for agriculture, allied activities, trade and services.

Table 4.8: Sectorwise Advances during 2007 to 2011

(Rs in Crore)

Category/ Year	SBI & Associates	Nationalised Banks	Public Sector Banks	Old Private Sector Banks	New Private Sector Banks	Foreign Banks
2007	371679	734608	1106288	82957	230005	97562
2008	482270	957877	1440146	92887	321865	126339
2009	593722	1203678	1797401	111670	406733	161133
2010	739450	1519762	2259212	128504	446824	165385
2011	858198	1843102	2701300	154136	478358	163260
CGAR %	62.21	69.87	67.32	43.33	51.09	34.86
Mean	609063.80	1251805.40	1860869.40	114030.80	376757.00	142735.80
S.D.	194763.95	440918.28	635497.82	28443.43	100846.40	29925.80
C.V.	31.98	35.22	34.15	24.94	26.77	20.97
Skew.	0.13	0.30	0.25	0.51	-0.77	-1.09

Source: Statistical Tables Related to Banks in India Various Issues, RBI Publication.

The above table gives the details of sectorwise advances made during 2005-06 to 2009-10. It is obvious that the sectorwise advances marks positive trend for all the sectors during the study period. The advances made by SBI & Associates, have increased from 3,71,679 to 8,58,198 crores, Nationalised Banks from 7,34,608 to 18,43,102 crores and the Public sector banks from 11,06,288 to 27,01,300 crores. Table 4.8 reveals that the nationalised banks have given maximum variation when compared to other sectors. All the sectors of banks have registered positive growth and skewed during the study period. Except New Private Sector banks and Foreign banks, the advances made by Old Private Sector banks have almost doubled. The Foreign banks were also served comparatively better during the period.

4.3.9. Growth of Interest Income

Total income of banks comprises of interest income and non-interest income. Interest income is considered to be an important source of income for financial companies. This is also otherwise called as net interest margin out of different categories of lending policies.

Table 4.9: Sectorwise Interest Income during 2007 to 2011

(Rs in Crore)

Category/ Year	SBI & Associates	Nationalised Banks	Public Sector Banks	Old Private Sector Banks	New Private Sector Banks	Foreign Banks
2007	49301	88574	137874	10372	24851	12291
2008	53465	110720	164185	11474	38092	17924
2009	70428	142647	213075	14614	56377	24417
2010	89196	183892	273088	18790	66282	30322
2011	97954	208535	306488	20565	62310	26389
CGAR %	54.34	66.72	62.42	53.53	73.47	60.46
Mean	72068.80	146873.60	218942.00	15163.00	49582.40	22268.60
S.D.	21392.47	49740.03	71064.87	4449.73	17540.71	7156.79
C.V.	29.68	33.87	32.46	29.35	35.38	32.14
Skew.	0.18	0.13	0.15	0.21	-0.74	-0.54

Source: Statistical Tables Related to Banks in India Various Issues, RBI Publication.

In the table 4.9 the sectorwise interest income describes positive trend for all the sectors during the study period. In SBI & Associates, it has increased from 49,301 to 97,954 crores, in the case of Nationalised Banks its has increased from 88,574 to 2,08,535 crores, in the case of Public sector banks it has increased from 1,37,874 to 3,06,488 crores and it reached to 20,565 from 10,372 crores in old private sector banks and it reached to 26,389 in foreign banks from 12,291 crores over a period of five years. Table 4.9 reveals that the new private sector bank has projected a maximum variation when compared to other sectors. The table also shows that excepting Private and Foreign banks all the sectors in the sample are positively skewed.

4.3.10. Growth of Other Income

Since, the interest income has been declining due to reform measures, banks had to take steps to increase non-interest income by enlarging their services. Non-interest income consists of Commission, exchange and Brokerage, Profit on sale of investments (net), Profit on revaluation of investments, Profit/loss on sale of land, buildings and other assets, Profit on exchange transactions (net) and Miscellaneous however, forms 15 percentage of the total income of the banks. With the deregulation of interest rates, banks are finding it tough to earn steady income from interest sources. Thus, this made banks in India to diversify their activities.

Table 4.10: Sectorwise Other Income during 2007 to 2011

(Rs in Crore)

Category/ Year	SBI & Associates	Nationalised Banks	Public Sector Banks	Old Private Sector Banks	New Private Sector Banks	Foreign Banks
2007	9526	12379	21905	1221	6870	5371
2008	9420	14264	23684	1568	10745	7044
2009	11818	20979	32797	2184	14822	10588
2010	16073	26394	42466	2782	15078	14894
2011	18394	29994	48388	3084	17095	9951
CGAR %	53.11	73.19	64.77	74.84	64.51	57.83
Mean	13046.20	20802.00	33848.00	2167.80	12922.00	9569.60
S.D.	4025.24	7574.41	11540.45	786.31	4093.85	3658.51
C.V.	30.85	36.41	34.09	36.27	31.68	38.23
Skew.	0.56	0.07	0.26	-0.05	-0.86	0.53

Source: Statistical Tables Related to Banks in India Various Issues, RBI Publication.

Table 4.10 shows the sectorwise capital reserves and surplus which is positive for all the sectors during the study period. In SBI & Associates, it has increased from 9,526 to 18,394 crores; in the case of Nationalised Banks its has increased from 12,379 to 29,994; in the case of Public sector banks it has increased from 21,905 to 48,388 crores it reached to 3,084 from 1,221 crores in old private sector banks and It reached to 9,951 crores from 5,371 crores in foreign banks over a period of five years. Table 4.10 reveals that the foreign banks have given maximum variation when compared to other sectors. Here, all the sectors of banks have shown positive growth during the study period. The table also shows that all the sectors in the sample are positively skewed except new private sector banks.

4.3.11. Growth of Interest Expended

Interest expended is related to providing better interest on deposits to different categories of depositors. Banks market policies are quite effective when the interest expended not exceeded the net interest margin.

Table 4.11: Sectorwise Interest Expended during 2007 to 2011

(Rs in Crore)

Category/ Year	SBI & Associates	Nationalised Banks	Public Sector Banks	Old Private Sector Banks	New Private Sector Banks	Foreign Banks
2007	28040	52464	80504	6247	15261	5149
2008	32607	69353	101960	7055	25802	7603
2009	47809	101093	148902	9960	38535	10604
2010	61770	131676	193447	12834	44123	12819
2011	66229	145712	211940	14076	37130	8938
CGAR %	72.1	80.98	66.84	66.84	70.4	45.39
Mean	47291.00	100059.60	147350.60	10034.40	32170.20	9022.60
S.D.	16991.02	39664.35	56630.05	3442.35	11559.14	2912.93
C.V.	35.93	39.64	38.43	34.31	35.93	32.28
Skew.	-0.04	-0.07	-0.06	0.07	-0.81	-0.04

Source: Statistical Tables Related to Banks in India Various Issues, RBI Publication.

Table 4.11 reveals the sectorwise interest expended for all the sectors during the study period. In SBI & Associates, it has increased from 28,040 to 66,229 crores; in the case of Nationalised Banks its has increased from 52,464 to 1,45,712 crores; in the case of Public sector banks it has increased from 80,504 to 2,11,940 crores, It reached to 14,076 from 6,247 crores in old private sector banks and it reached to 8,938 crores in foreign banks from 5,149 crores over a period of five years. Table 4.11 reveals that the Nationalsied banks have given maximum variation when compared to other sectors. Here, all the sectors of banks have shown positive growth during the study period. The table also shows that all the sectors in the sample are negatively skewed except Old Private Sector banks.

4.3.12. Operating Expenses

Operating expenses per branch includes establishment expenses, rent taxes, lighting, printing and stationery, advertisement and publicity, depreciation etc., It is the expenditure incurred to operate a branch. When viewed at the average operating expenditure per branch, there is an increase in it over the period.

Table 4.12: Sectorwise Operating Expenses during 2007 to 2011

(Rs in Crore)

Category/ Year	SBI & Associates	Nationalised Banks	Public Sector Banks	Old Private Sector Banks	New Private Sector Banks	Foreign Banks
2007	15760	25548	41308	3089	8949	5854
2008	15987	27268	43255	2967	12353	7745
2009	16993	29670	46663	3235	17032	10353
2010	20088	35416	55504	3939	17840	12298
2011	25199	40792	65991	4715	17960	11102
CGAR %	30.82	31.74	31.4	29.64	49.99	49.36
Mean	18805.40	31738.80	50544.20	3589.00	14826.80	9470.40
S.D.	3969.44	6286.42	10206.70	733.58	4013.34	2621.63
C.V.	21.11	19.81	20.19	20.44	27.07	27.68
Skew.	1.38	0.77	1.01	1.12	-0.96	-0.57

Source: Statistical Tables Related to Banks in India Various Issues, RBI Publication.

The table 4.12 shows increased operating expenses of all sectors of banks during the study period. No sector is exceptional to this. This may be due to the reason that banks have to open as many branches as they can to compete with others. The increased establishment charges also contribute much towards operating expenses. By the introduction of LPG, foreign banks are freely allowed to open branch in our country and our banks are opening branches in foreign soil as well. This may cause the increased operating expenses in almost all sectors.

4.3.13. Cost of Funds

The rising cost of funds may put bank margins under pressure. The increasing cost of deposits may hit net interest margin of banks. The heavy competition among banks limits the ability to pass on the rise in the cost of funds to customers. Cost of funds is also the rate of interest that a borrower have to pay in order to obtain money through a loan. It can also be referred to as the cost of borrowing money.

Table 4.13: Sectorwise Cost of Funds during 2007 to 2011

(Rs in Crore)

Category/ Year	SBI & Associates	Nationalised Banks	Public Sector Banks	Old Private Sector Banks	New Private Sector Banks	Foreign Banks
2007	4.84	4.27	4.46	4.77	4.14	3.63
2008	4.75	4.80	4.79	4.98	5.24	4.03
2009	5.90	5.82	5.85	6.20	6.11	4.33
2010	5.94	6.09	6.04	6.67	6.06	4.46
2011	5.32	5.35	5.34	6.13	4.43	2.82
CGAR %	9.96	17.19	14.6	20.05	6.67	-8.87
Mean	5.35	5.27	5.30	5.75	5.20	3.85
S.D.	0.56	0.74	0.67	0.83	0.91	0.66
C.V.	10.54	14.09	12.73	14.41	17.44	17.13
Skew.	0.05	-0.37	-0.18	-0.35	-0.12	-1.13

Source: Statistical Tables Related to Banks in India Various Issues, RBI Publication.

From the table 4.13, it is clear that the sectorwise cost of funds shows positive trend for all the sectors during the study period except for foreign banks. In SBI & Associates, it has increased from 15,760 to 25,199; in the case of Nationalised Banks its has increased from 25,548 to 40,792 and in the case of Public sector banks it has increased from 41,308 to 65,991. It reached to 4,715 from 3,089 in old private sector banks and it reached to 11,102 in foreign banks from 5,854 over a period of five years. Table 4.13 reveals that the foreign banks have given maximum variation when compared to other sectors. Here, all the sectors of banks have shown positive growth during the study period. The table also shows that all the sectors in the sample are negatively skewed except SBI & Associates.

4.3.14. Return on Advances Adjusted to COF

Cost of funds shows the liability of the banks for the financing which they had undergone. To improve the profit margin it should always be on the lower side. Return on Advances is computed by dividing the total interest earned by banks on their advances by the total amount of advances. So, a higher RoA indicates a better earning capacity of the bank or the group concerned.

Table 4.14: Sectorwise Return on Advances Adjusted to COF during 2007 to 2011

(Rs in Crore)

Category/ Year	SBI & Associates	Nationalised Banks	Public Sector Banks	Old Private Sector Banks	New Private Sector Banks	Foreign Banks
2007	2.93	3.86	3.55	3.95	4.58	4.90
2008	3.72	3.99	3.90	4.06	4.47	5.74
2009	3.65	3.69	3.67	4.26	5.05	6.60
2010	3.95	4.09	4.04	5.15	5.23	8.14
2011	3.60	3.83	3.76	4.81	5.13	7.17
CGAR %	11.47	0.21	3.51	15.65	9.24	29.14
Mean	3.57	3.89	3.78	4.45	4.89	6.51
S.D.	0.38	0.15	0.19	0.51	0.34	1.25
C.V.	10.70	3.95	5.07	11.57	7.02	19.26
Skew.	-1.52	0.02	0.24	0.65	-0.51	0.00

Source: Statistical Tables Related to Banks in India Various Issues, RBI Publication.

From the table 4.14, it is obvious that the sector wise Return on Advances Adjusted to COF shows positive trend for all the sectors during the study period. In SBI & Associates, it has increased from 2.93 to 3.60; in the case of Nationalised Banks its has increased from 3.86 to 3.83; and in the case of Public sector banks it has increased from 3.55 to 3.76. It reached to 4.81 from 3.95 in old private sector banks and it reached to 7.17 in foreign banks from 4.90 over a period of five years. Table 4.14 reveals that the foreign banks have given maximum variation when compared to other sectors. Here, all the sectors of banks have shown positive growth during the study period. The table also shows that all the sectors in the sample are positively skewed except SBI & Associates and foreign banks.

4.3.15. Wages as Percentage to Total Expenses

Public sector banks spent about a quarter of their total operating expenses towards employee cost. But over the last four years, these banks have managed to keep these expenses under control, large scale retirement that led to an overall contraction of public sector banks' cumulative manpower. Private banks are known to be better paymasters. That private banks employ a much lower headcount obviously helps them keep the ratio well below their public sector counterparts is common knowledge. Profitability of public sector banks has been on the rise. There is a corresponding rise in total expenses, too, to support high profitability.

Table 4.15: Sectorwise Wages as Percentage to Total Expenses during 2007 to 2011

(Rs in Crore)

Category/ Year	SBI & Associates	Nationalised Banks	Public Sector Banks	Old Private Sector Banks	New Private Sector Banks	Foreign Banks
2007	24.35	21.42	22.48	18.93	9.54	18.22
2008	21.55	17.94	19.15	16.89	9.36	20.08
2009	15.89	14.05	14.66	13.67	9.56	19.95
2010	15.06	13.31	13.88	13.26	10.17	19.44
2011	17.03	13.65	14.76	14.57	12.14	23.48
CGAR %	-21.89	-24.13	-23.49	-16.16	13.89	11.55
Mean	18.78	16.07	16.99	15.46	10.15	20.23
S.D.	4.00	3.52	3.70	2.39	1.15	1.96
C.V.	21.30	21.92	21.81	15.48	11.34	9.67
Skew.	0.74	1.10	1.00	0.83	1.88	1.42

Source: Statistical Tables Related to Banks in India Various Issues, RBI Publication.

Table 4.15 shows the percentage of wages to total expenses during the period 2005-06 to 2009-10. It considerably reduced in all the sectors due to automation and mechanisation. From the above table it is observed that excepting foreign banks, all the sectors have minimised this component. Extensive use of net banking, e-banking, funds transfer etc. minimise the visit of the customers to banks. The new banking policy allows merger and takeover of banks by other banks whereby the dependence on man power is considerably reduced. This is another reason for the reduction in percentage of wages to their employees which reduces the percentage wages to total expenses. The wage in public sector banks has shrunk to below 15% in 2009-10 from 22% in 2005-06. For the private banks cluster, this ratio is even lower at 10%. Eventhough private banks are known to be better performers, they employ less numbers of employees which helps them keep the ratio well below their public sector counterparts.

4.3.16. Return on Assets

An indicator of profitability of a company is to total assets. ROA gives an idea as to how efficient management is at using its assets to generate earnings. Calculated by dividing a bank's annual earnings by its total assets, ROA is displayed as a percentage. Return on assets is a common figure used for comparing performance of financial institutions (such as banks), because the majority of their assets will have a carrying value that is close to their actual market value. Return on assets is not useful for comparisons between industries because of factors of scale and peculiar capital requirements (such as reserve requirements in the insurance and banking industries).

Table 4.16: Sectorwise Return on Assets during 2007 to 2011

(Rs in Crore)

Category/ Year	SBI & Associates	Nationalised Banks	Public Sector Banks	Old Private Sector Banks	New Private Sector Banks	Foreign Banks
2007	0.87	0.89	0.88	0.64	1.22	2.08
2008	0.86	0.94	0.92	0.78	1.09	2.28
2009	0.97	1.01	1.00	1.14	1.13	2.09
2010	1.02	1.03	1.03	1.15	1.12	1.99
2011	0.91	1.00	0.97	0.95	1.38	1.26
CGAR %	6.18	7.75	7.34	31.16	6.5	-23.06
Mean	0.93	0.97	0.96	0.93	1.19	1.94
S.D.	0.07	0.06	0.06	0.22	0.12	0.39
C.V.	7.35	5.92	6.29	23.96	9.91	20.34
Skew.	0.59	-0.85	-0.32	-0.34	1.44	-1.82

Source: Statistical Tables Related to Banks in India Various Issues, RBI Publication.

The table 4.16 shows that the return on assets of banks for the period from 2005-06 to 2009-10. A good metric for evaluating banks performance is the banks' return on assets. While calculating ROA, banks are highly leveraged. ROA gives investor a reliable picture of management's ability to pull profit from the assets. All sectors saw a fall in their return on asset during 2009-10 period. ROA is a good internal management ratio because it measures profit against all assets a bank uses to make those earnings. In all sectors, the ROA has increased and showed a positive trend during the study period.

4.3.17. Capital to Risk Assets Ratio (CRAR)

As the name indicates that the capital conservative buffer can be dipped during stressed period to meet the minimum regulatory requirement on core capital. In this scenario, the bank would not be supposed to use its earnings to make discretionary payouts such as dividends, shares buyback, etc. The counter cyclical buffer, achieved through a pro-cyclical build up of the buffer in good times, is expected to protect the banking industry from system-wide risks arising out of excessive aggregate credit growth.

Table 4.17: Sectorwise CRAR during 2007 to 2011

(Rs in Crore)

Category/ Year	SBI & Associates	Nationalised Banks	Public Sector Banks	Old Private Sector Banks	New Private Sector Banks	Foreign Banks
2007	11.95	12.27	12.17	11.69	12.60	13.02
2008	12.30	12.37	12.36	12.08	11.99	12.39
2009	13.21	12.13	12.51	14.08	14.39	13.08
2010	13.96	13.24	13.49	14.76	15.33	14.32
2011	13.46	13.25	13.32	15.21	17.96	17.25
CGAR %	8.75	5.23	6.36	18.21	24.58	17.69
Mean	12.98	12.65	12.77	13.56	14.45	14.01
S.D.	0.83	0.55	0.60	1.59	2.38	1.94
C.V.	6.41	4.33	4.66	11.73	16.43	13.85
Skew.	-0.22	0.50	0.47	-0.37	0.70	1.59

Source: Statistical Tables Related to Banks in India Various Issues, RBI Publication.

From the table 4.17, it is clear that the sector wise CRAR shows positive trend for all the sectors during the study period except for foreign banks. In SBI & Associates, it has increased from 11.95 to 13.46; in the case of Nationalised Banks its has increased from 12.27 to 13.25 and in the case of Public sector banks it has increased from 12.17 to 13.32. It reached to 15.21 from 11.69 in old private sector banks and it reached to 17.25 from 13.02 in foreign banks over a period of five years. Table 4.17 reveals that the new private sector banks have given maximum variation when compared to other sectors. The table also shows that all the sectors in the sample are positively skewed except SBI & Associates and old private sector banks.

4.3.18. Net NPA Ratio

NPA is defined as an advance for which interest or repayment of principal or both remain outstanding for a period of more than two quarters. The level of NPA is acting as an indicator showing the banker's credit risks and efficiency of allocation of resource. Loans and advances given by banks to its customers is an asset to the bank. But, when repayment of interest and Principal is overdue, such asset is classified as NPA in the financial reports of banks. The Indian banking sector is facing a serious problem of NPA. The extent of NPA is comparatively higher in public sectors banks. To improve the efficiency and profitability, the NPA has to be scheduled. Various steps have been taken by the government to reduce the NPA. It is highly impossible to have zero percentage NPA. But at least Indian banks can try competing with foreign banks to maintain international standard.

Table 4.18: Sectorwise Net NPA Ratio during 2007 to 2011

(Rs in Crore)

Category/ Year	SBI & Associates	Nationalised Banks	Public Sector Banks	Old Private Sector Banks	New Private Sector Banks	Foreign Banks
2007	1.63	1.16	1.32	1.66	0.78	0.83
2008	1.32	0.94	1.06	0.96	0.97	0.73
2009	1.43	0.77	0.99	0.66	1.21	0.77
2010	1.47	0.68	0.94	0.90	1.40	1.81
2011	1.50	0.91	1.10	0.83	1.09	1.82
CGAR %	-1.34	-0.17	-10.56	-28.39	26.94	76.94
Mean	1.47	0.89	1.08	1.00	1.09	1.19
S.D.	0.11	0.18	0.15	0.38	0.24	0.57
C.V.	7.65	20.54	13.56	38.38	21.56	47.81
Skew.	0.20	0.54	1.30	1.75	0.00	0.59

Source: Statistical Tables Related to Banks in India Various Issues, RBI Publication.

The net NPA ratio of public sector banks and old private sector banks declined, while it increased for new private sector and foreign banks. In almost all sectors of banks, the NPA ratio is less than 2%. The NPA ratio of foreign banks and new private sector banks witnessed significant increase indicating deteriorating asset quality of these banks on account of slowing economic activity following the global economic crisis. By certain relaxation permitted to banks by RBI, the net NPA increased during 2009-10. It signifies the need for better risk management to avoid decrease in asset quality.

4.4. Relationship between Bank Level Variables and Agricultural Credit by Commercial Banks

Independent India started with a weak financial system. Commercial banks mobilized household savings through demand and term deposits, and disbursed the credit primarily to large corporations after independence. The main thrust of nationalization was social banking with the stated objective of increasing the geographical coverage of the banking system and extension of credit to the priority sector that comprised largely of agriculture, agro-processing, and small-scale industries. This phase of banking in India was characterized by administered interest rates, mandatory syndicated lending and pre-emption of the banks' deposit base by the government in the form of measures like high Cash Reserve Ratio (CRR) and Statutory Liquidity Ratio (SLR). Banks were required to invest a significant proportion of their deposits in bonds issued by the government and "approved" (quasi-government) institutions.[1]

---

[1]Bhaumik, Piesse, (2008), "Does lending behaviour of banks in emerging economies vary by ownership? Evidence from the Indian banking sector", *Economic Systems*, 32, Pp.177–196.

Credit delivery to the agriculture sector continues to be inadequate. The Indian banking system is still hesitant on various grounds to purvey credit to small and marginal farmers. Credit, as one of the critical non-land inputs, has two-dimensions from the viewpoint of its contribution to the augmentation of agricultural growth *viz.*, availability of credit (the quantum) and the distribution of credit[1]. This part focused only on commercial banks to reveal the effect of bank level variables in determining the agriculture credit by commercial banks.

4.5. Predicted relationship between Bank Characteristics and Institutional Credit to Agriculture

Size of the Bank ($SIZE_{it}$)

Bank organization size is represented through the sum of total of all the assets of banks which includes all the branches. In India, there is no single bank holding company as in USA. This study took number of branches to measure the SIZE of the different categories of banks. Increasing number of branches also trigger the bank credit level because each has to show its record in credit disbursal. Small banks encounter more asymmetric information problems in the capital market than large banks and therefore, they may find it difficult to raise uninsured (i.e., non-deposit) funds in response to monetary tightening.

Return on Assets (ROA_{it})

Return on Assets is considered as a measure for bank profitability. Higher profitability in the banking sector is due to lower cost of funds or high loan rates. There is a lack of evidence on how ROA influences agriculture loan of a bank. In India, directed credit may play a role in influencing return but banking sector left with no alternative other than in showing strong financial position. There is a general belief that ROA is an indication of stronger financial position which may positively influence the credit towards agriculture. Liquid banks can draw on their reserves of cash and securities to protect their loan portfolio, while this is less possible for illiquid banks.

Cost of Funds (COF_{it})

Cost of funds is considered as one of the strong measures and an indicator of fund efficiency. Cost of funds is a determinant of profitability and can affect lending policies. If a

[1]Ramesh Golait (2007), "Current Issues in Agriculture Credit in India: An Assessment", *Reserve Bank of India Occasional Papers*, 28, 1, summer.

bank is profitable due to low cost of fund, it may be more willing to serve only the potential customers. This implies the negative relationship between priority credit to agriculture sector and cost of fund of a bank. Economies of scale in this process are expected to help banks to economise on costs. Indirectly, this process would help improve banking habits and lead to increase in the savings of the household sector. In India, in 1950s and the early 1960s , some of the small banks were consolidated under the guidance of the RBI to economise the costs.

Risk Level ($RISK_{it}$)

Adverse selection occurs in the credit market when lenders provide funds to projects that do not give assured viability, hoping that projects will succeed over time with some assumed or promised actions on the part of borrowers. It could also occur when banks, not fully aware of the different risks that borrowers carry, provide funds at high interest rates in order to improve banks expected profits. Banks could use collaterals such as real estate as screening device.

Capital Adequacy Ratio (CAR_{it})

Poorly capitalized banks have less access to non-deposit funds and therefore, are forced to cut back their loan supply by more than well capitalised banks [Peek and Rosengren 1995[1]; Kishan and Opiela 2000][2]. It is documented that well capitalized banks acted as a boosting factor for lending during unfavorable economic conditions.

Non Performing Assets Ratio (NPA_{it})

A classification used by financial institutions that refers to loans that are in threat of default. Once the borrower has failed to make interest or principal payments for 90 days the loan is considered to be a non-performing asset. Non-performing assets are problematic for financial institutions since they depend on interest payments for income. Worrying pressure from the economy can lead to a sharp increase in non-performing loans and often results in massive writedowns.

4.6. Panel Data Empirical Framework

Several articles focused on the need for banking sector to consider improving their lending schemes. The existing bank level data shows that banks are not sufficiently supporting the

---

[1]Joe Peek & Eric S. Rosengren, 1995. "*Small business credit availability: how important is size of lender?*," Working Papers 95-5, Federal Reserve Bank of Boston.

[2]Kishan, R. P. and Opiela, T. P. (2000), 'Bank size, bank capital, and the bank lending channel', *Journal of Money, Credit and Banking*, 32,1, Pp. 121–41.

priority sector lending, which in turn is going to have big impact on the agricultural sector itself. The factors like branch operations, number of branches in rural areas, financial inclusion and its impact, credit deposit ratio, lending policies, RBI policy, sectoral development and other factors are analyzed with empirical evidence and statistical relevance.[1]

This study considers the above discussed measures to find the effect of bank variables on the agriculture credit by commercial banks. Brailsford et. al[2] (2002) employed OLS regression assuming that the unobservable individual effect on the selected firms as Zero. However in India, firms are heterogeneous especially in financing decisions which is common across firms within the same group. Therefore there is a need for applying panel data econometric models for better empirical estimation by considering individual bank heterogeneity. Panel data takes care of collinearity among the explanatory variables and thus improving the precision of econometric results (Psillaki and Daskalakis, 2008)[3].

Total data set is classified and regression model is employed as given below:

$$AC_{it} = \alpha + \beta_1 ROA_{it} + \beta_2 SIZE_{it} + \beta_3 COF_{it} + \beta_4 RISK_{it} + \beta_5 CAR_{it} + \beta_6 NPA_{it} + \mu \text{....(1)}$$

Where,

AC_{it} is the agricultural credit of a bank *i* over the period *t*.

ROA_{it} is the return on assets of a bank *i* over the period *t*

$SIZE_{it}$ is the number of total branches a bank *i* over the period *t*.

COF_{it} is the is the cost of funds of a bank *i* over the period *t*

$RISK_{it}$ is the standard deviation of earnings of a bank *i* over the period *t*.

CAR_{it} is the capital to assets ratio of a bank *i* over the period *t*.

NPA_{it} is the non performance assets of a bank *i* over the period *t*.

μ_{it} is the error term.

This study employs panel data estimation model to capture a dynamic relationship that exists between bank characteristics and credit flow to agriculture from a bank. The data set used for the analysis is pooled across banks and years, given unbalanced panel data set of ten bank years' observation. The traditional panel data model includes three different methods: a) Common Constant Method, b) Fixed Effects Method, and c) Random Effects Method. In this

[1]Subramaniam and Ravi Subramaniam (2009), "Role of Banks in Agricultural lending-India", *http://ssrn.com/abstract=1483243.*

[2]Brailsford, Oliver, and Pua, (2002). On the Relation between Ownership Structure and Capital Structure. *Accounting and Finance*, 42, 1-26.

[3]Psilikkai, and Daskalialias, (2008). Are the Determinants of Capital Structure Country or Firm Specific? *Small Business Economics*, Springer Business Media.

study, the researcher incorporates all these methods to analyse the robustness of parameter coefficients in explaining the relationship between equity ownership holding and debt level. The common constant method is the usual pooled ordinary least square method. It also implies that there is no difference between the estimated cross-sections and it is useful under the hypothesis that the data set is a *priori* homogeneous. However, this case is quite restrictive and case of more interest involves the inclusion of fixed and Random Effects in the method of estimation.[1]

The Fixed Effects Model (FEM) and Random Effects Models (REM) are the classical tests for panel data analysis. The Fixed Effects Method treats the constant as group (section)-specific, i.e. it allows for different constants for each group (section) and it includes a dummy variable for each group and the functional form is as, $Y_{it} = (\alpha + \mu_i) + X_{it}' \beta + V_{it}$. The REM assumes that there is a single common intercept term, but that the intercepts for individual firms vary from this common intercept in a random manner and the Functional form is written as, $Y_{it} = \alpha + X'_{it} \beta + (\mu_i + V_{it})$.

Fixed effects are tested by the (incremental) F test, while random effects are examined by the Lagrange Multiplier (LM) test (Breusch and Pagan, 1980)[2]. If the null hypothesis is not rejected, the pooled OLS regression is favored. The Hausman specification test[3] compares Fixed Effect and Random Effect models. In general,The Hausman test is a test for the null hypothesis of no correlation where a small value of the Hausman statistic implies that the random effects model is more appropriate estimator. The Hausman test checks a more efficient model against a less efficient but consistent model to make sure that the more efficient model also gives consistent results. This test tests the null hypothesis that the coefficients estimated by the random effects estimator are the same as the ones estimated by the fixed effects estimator. If they are insignificant (P-value, Prob>chi^2 larger than .05) then it is better to use random effects.

This table 4.19 presents the results of panel data model to capture the relationship between bank level variables and agricultural credit for a sample of commercial banks. The panel data model includes common constant method, Fixed Effects Method and Random Effects Method; these results are presented in Panel A, Panel B and Panel C respectively. The dependent variable is Agricultural credit.

---

[1]Asterio D and S Price (2006), *"Applied Econometrics'*, A Modern Approach. Palgrave Macmillan.

[2]Breusch T S and Pagan A R, 1980. "The Lagrange Multiplier Test and Its Applications to Model Specification in Econometrics," *Review of Economic Studies*, Wiley Blackwell, 47, 1, Pp. 239-53.

[3]Hausman, J. A. (1978). Specification tests in econometrics, *Econometrica*, 46, 6, Pp.1251– 1272.

4.7. Results and Discussion

Table 4.19: Base Line Panel Data Estimates for Bank Characteristics and Credit Flow to Agriculture

	Panel A		Panel B		Panel C	
Variables	**Common Constant Method**		**Fixed Effects Method**		**Random Effects Method**	
	Co.ef.	**t value**	**Co.ef.**	**t value**	**Co.ef.**	**t value**
ROA	0.261	6.51*	0.211	4.81*	0.251	6.39*
SIZE	0.004	0.35	0.281	1.98**	0.018	1.49
COF	-0.950	-9.70*	-0.906	-6.53*	-0.959	-7.80*
RISK	-1.196	-7.49*	-0.593	-4.39*	-0.614	-4.65*
CAR	0.032	2.81*	0.012	1.10	0.017	1.59
NPA	-0.123	-4.66*	-0.136	-2.12**	-0.014	-1.32
Adj R^2	0.462		0.323		0.447	
F (Incre), Chi^2			20.14 (0.000)			
L.M(Prob> Chi^2)					45.13 (0.000)	
Hausman t-value			54.03 (0.000)			

** denote significant at 0.05 levels; * denote significant at 0.01 level, ROA: Return on assets of a bank; SIZE: Natural log of total assets; COF: Cost of funds of a bank; RISK: S.D. of earnings of a bank; CAR: Capital to assets ratio; NPA: Non-performing assets to total assets.

The empirical estimates of Fixed Effects Model reveals the relationship between the credit flow to agriculture and variables of selected banks are presented in Panel B of Table-4.19. The ROA is the profitability of the bank having positive relationship with the credit to agriculture in a significant way. This gives support to the argument that lending increases with profitability of commercial banks (Bhaumik, 2001)[1]. This is consistent with the existing argument that the profitability is generally positively correlated with bank lending (Thakor, 1996; Jackson et al., 1999).[2] SIZE of the bank also has positive relationship with the credit to agriculture. This confirms the argument that big size banks are less prone to financial distress (Bhaduri, 2002)[3]. This also suggests that commercial banks lend more if they have greater ability to absorb adverse shocks by way of loan defaults and big Size.

The Cost of Funds (COF) and Risk level (RISK) are having the negatively significant relationship with the credit to agriculture. This leads to the argument that the excess cost of fund may be the credit to different sectors especially directed credit. If firms are not stable in their earnings capacity, risky loans are not avoided but postponed in the case of directed

[1]Bhaumik, S.K., Piesse, J., 2008.Op.Cit.

[2]Jackson, Patricia, and Craig Furfine, Hans Groeneveld, Diana Hancock, David Jones, William Perraudin, Lawrence Radecki, Masao Yoneyama (1999). "Capital Requirements and Bank Behaviour: The Impact of the Basle Accord." *Basle Committee on Banking Supervision Working Papers*, 1, April.

[3]Bhaduri, N.S. (2002). Determinants of Corporate Borrowing: Some Evidence from Indian Corporate Structure. *Journal of Economics and Finance*, 26, Pp. 200-215.

credit. One of the prudential characteristics, Capital Adequacy Norms (CAR) shows statistically insignificant relationship with the dependent variable, though the co - efficient value is negative. The non performing assets ratio shows negative relationship with the credit to agriculture. Negative relationship confirms that banks reacting negatively towards overdues. The coefficient of variation adjusted R^2 is high of 32.3 percentage charging the variation in credit flow to agriculture which is strongly explained by the variations of bank level characteristic and other attributes.

4.8. Sectorwise Classification for Commercial Banks

This section tries to answer whether different types of banks have shown any notable result in lending to agriculture. As similar to the base line equation, for different types of banks the equation was formed.

A. SBI and its Associates

After the nationalization of fourteen commercial banks in 1969, banking had largely been a state dominated activity in India. Subsequently in 1980, six more banks were nationalized. Of these public sector banks, State Bank of India and seven of its associate banks, with earlier history of state control, are perhaps a class by itself. The Imperial Bank of India which was the conversion of Presidency Banks was nationalized in 1955. Together they constituted the state controlled public sector banks accounting for more than three fourth of total assets, in which the share of SBI alone was one fourth (Ray, 2008)[1].

B. Nationalised Banks

Nationalised banks differ largely in size and at one end line of the spectrum, there are large banks like Punjab National Bank or Bank of Baroda and at the other end there are small banks like Vijaya Bank. An interesting feature of nationalized is that they listed in the stock exchanges with number of them assessed the equity market. The initial infusion of capital by the government in public sector banks was followed by expanding the capital base with equity participation by the private investors. The nationalised banks in India are not fully government owned and there are elements of private ownership in them. This mixed ownership interest is an important feature of bank governance in India (Mohan, 2004).[2]

[1]Ray (2008), Op.Cit.

[2]Mohan, Rakesh (2004): "Agricultural Credit in India: Status, Issues and Future Agenda", *RBI Bulletin, November.*

C. Private Banks

There are large number of private sector banks in India. After the nationalization of fourteen commercial banks in 1969, no new private banks were licensed by the RBI in the country until the early 1990s though there was no legal barrier on the entry of private sector banks. However, since 1990s, expectedly their share increased since the mid 1990s with the initiation of financial liberalization in India. Old generation private banks started out and continue to function as community banks. To begin with they were nurtured and developed by particular communities. Most of these banks have nearly 75 percentage of their branches in the state they were found in. A large number of banks were founded in Tamil Nadu and Kerala; 10 such banks operate in both these states. New private sector banks have not set up in India till 1993. The Narashiman committee report of 1991 has envisaged a larger role for private sector banks in recognition of the need to introduce greater competition with a view to achieving higher productivity and efficiency of the banking system in India. In order to introduce greater competition in the banking system, the RBI issued guidelines in January 1993 for the establishment of new banks in the private sector.

The table 4.20 presents the results of panel data model to capture the relationship between bank level variables and agricultural credit for a sample of commercial banks based on sectoral differentiation. The panel data model includes Common Constant Method, Fixed Effects Method and Random Effects Method; these results are presented in Panel A, Panel B and Panel C respectively. The dependent variable is Agricultural credit.

Table 4.20: Sector wise Panel data estimates for Bank Level Variables and Credit flow to Agriculture

	Panel A		**Panel B**		**Panel C**	
Variables	**SBI & Associates**		**Nationalized Banks**		**Private Banks**	
	Co.ef.	t value	Co.ef.	t value	Co.ef.	t value
ROA	0.557	5.32*	0.519	2.43**	0.027	1.02
SIZE	1.668	2.56*	0.012	3.81*	0.094	6.75*
COF	-1.150	-1.14	-0.262	-2.35**	-1.371	-6.90*
RISK	-0.793	-1.47	-1.535	-3.26*	-0.614	-3.84*
CAR	0.048	0.09	0.762	1.59	0.081	4.30*
NPA	-0.292	-0.769	-0.317	-3.92*	-0.968	-1.21
Adj R^2	0.212		0.319		0.466	
F (Incre), Chi^2			20.14 (0.000)			
L.M(Prob> Chi^2)					45.13 (0.000)	
Hausman t-value			54.03 (0.000)			

** denote significant at 0.05 levels; *denote significant at 0.01 level, ROA: Return on assets of a bank; SIZE: Natural log of total assets; COF: Cost of funds of a bank; RISK: S.D. of earnings of a bank; CAR: Capital to assets ratio; NPA: Non-performing assets to total assets.

The empirical estimates of fixed effects model reveals the relationship between the credit flow to agriculture and variables of selected banks based on sector wise are presented in Panel B of Table-4.20. The ROA is the profitability of the bank having positive relationship with the credit to agriculture to all the selected sectors except for private banks in a significant way. This gives support to the argument that lending increases with profitability of commercial banks (Bhaumik, 2008)[1] but this might not work in the case of private banks. This is consistent with the existing argument that the profitability is generally positively correlated with bank lending but private banks may have more avenues to invest in a fruitful way than the agriculture sector. SIZE of the bank also has positive relationship with the credit to agriculture. This confirms the argument that big size banks are less prone to financial distress (Bhaduri, 2002).[2] This also suggests that commercial banks lend more if they have greater ability to absorb adverse shocks by way of loan defaults and big Size and this also consistent with the worked out base line results.

The cost of funds (COF) shows negatively significant relationship with the credit flow to agriculture by private banks and nationalized banks and strength of impact of COF on agriculture credit is comparatively lower for nationalized banks. The relationship between COF and credit flow to agriculture for the SBI & Associates are statistically in significant. Risk level (RISK) is having the negatively significant relationship with the credit to agriculture both for private banks and for nationalized banks. If firms are not stable in their earnings capacity, risky loans are not avoided but postponed in the case of directed credit. There is a insignificant relationship between RISK and credit flow to agriculture for SBI & its Associates.

Capital Adequacy Ratio (CAR) shows statistically significant relationship with the private sector banks and it shows insignificant relationship with the nationalized and SBI & its Associates. The non performing assets ratio shows negative relationship with the credit to agriculture and it is significant in the case of Nationalised banks. Negative relationship confirms that banks react negatively towards overdue but government may also stress some basic outlay to the agriculture. The coefficient of variation adjusted R^2 of private sector banks is quite high of 46.6 percentage which is comparatively higher than the remaining two sectors of banks which are also in the field of agriculture credit.

---

[1]Bhaumik, (2008), Op.Cit..

[2]Bhaduri, (2002), Op.Cit..

4.9. Sizewise Classification of Banks

Size of the bank is considered as one of the measurements for lending pattern. As far as Indian banks are concerned it is interestingly perceived that Size does matter. Large banks, are the banks with more capital or in terms of aggregate assets. Size tended to be an important factor which has been expressed in terms of aggregate assets.

The definition of Size is as follows[1]:

$$\text{Size} = S_{it} = \ln(\text{Assets})_{it}$$

The above said criteria is normalised with respect to their averages across all banks, so that they sum to zero over all observations. In the case of size, the normalisation is not just over the sample mean over the whole sample period, but over the means per year as well, so that trends in bank size are removed[2].

$$\text{Size}_{it} = \text{Log } A_{it} - \frac{\sum_{i} \text{Log } A_{it}}{N}$$

As far as Size is concerned, from the sample the Quartile 1 and Quartile 3 values for Size variables are arrived at 7.4651 and 10.6792, respectively. As stated, all banks for which S_{it} is less than Q1 are called as Small Banks. All banks for which S_{it} more than Q3 are termed as Large banks. Several prominent works have pointed out that large banks are able to insulate their portfolio from the contractionary monetary policy operations. In a nutshell this part discussed with how the normalized Size shows any significant result in lending to agriculture.

The table 4.21 presents the results of panel data model to capture the relationship between bank level variables and agricultural credit for a sample of 28 commercial banks based on Size differentiation. The panel data model includes Common Constant Method, Fixed Effects Method and Random Effects Method; these results are presented in Panel A, Panel B and Panel C respectively. The dependent variable is Agricultural credit.

---

[1]Prasad, A and S Ghosh (2005): 'Monetary Policy and Corporate Behaviour in India', IMF Working Paper No 25, Washington DC.

[2]Kishan, R P and T P Opiela (2000): 'Bank Size,Bank Capital and the Bank Lending Channel', *Journal of Money, Credit and Banking*, 32, pp 121-41.

Table 4.21: Size wise Panel data estimates for Bank Level Variables and Credit flow to Agriculture

	Panel A		Panel B	
Variables	Small Banks		Large Banks	
	Co.ef.	t value	Co.ef.	t value
ROA	0.050	2.26**	0.211	2.03**
SIZE	0.239	5.62*	0.281	3.27*
COF	-0.413	-2.38**	-0.006	-1.073
VOL	-0.358	-2.17**	-0.593	-3.40*
CAR	-0.081	-0.273	-0.012	-1.61
NPA	-0.645	-3.10*	-0.036	-2.69*
Adj R^2	0.522		0.608	
Model	Fixed Effects		Fixed Effects	

** denote significant at 0.05 levels; * denote significant at 0.01 level, ROA: Return on assets of a bank; SIZE: Natural log of total assets; COF: Cost of funds of a bank; RISK: S.D. of earnings of a bank; CAR: Capital to assets ratio; NPA: Non-performing assets to total assets.

The empirical estimates of Fixed Effects Model reveals the relationship between the credit flow to agriculture and variables of small and large banks are presented in Panel B of Table-4.21. The ROA is the profitability of the bank having significant positive relationship with the credit to agriculture to small banks as well as large banks. This has confirmed the argument that lending increases with profitability of commercial banks.

SIZE of the bank also has positive relationship with the credit to agriculture. This is consistent with the existing argument that the profitability is generally positively correlated with bank lending irrespective of the size. This confirms the argument that bigger banks and financial institutions are less prone to financial distress and there is less chance of bankruptcy. This also suggests that commercial banks lend more if the sizes of the assets are at the increasing trend. The Cost of Funds (COF) shows negative significant relationship with the credit flow to agriculture by small banks and in the case of large banks the strength of impact of COF on agriculture credit is statistically insignificant. Risk level (RISK) is having the negatively significant relationship with the credit to agriculture both for the small banks and for large banks. This leads to the argument that the fluctuation in the earnings discourages the directed credit which always focused on societal objective. If firms are not stable in their earning capacity, risky loans are not avoided but postponed in the case of directed credit. There is a insignificant relationship between RISK and credit flow to agriculture for all the banks irrespective of their size.

Capital Adequacy (CAR) shows statistically insignificant relationship with the all the size of banks but coefficient sign proves the negative relationship with the credit flow to agriculture.

The non performing assets ratio of small banks shows negative relationship with the credit to agriculture and it is insignificant in the case of large banks. Negative relationship confirms that banks reacting negatively towards overdue but government may also stress some basic outlay to the agriculture. The adjusted R^2 of small banks is quite high of 52.2 percentage which is comparatively higher than the large banks.

4.10. Conclusion

Although these developments have made institutions more efficient by lowering transaction costs, they have also challenged the traditional regulatory arrangements based on institutions. The heightened competitive pressures, by squeezing profit margins of institutions, could lead them to pursue riskier strategies, raising the possibility of failure. Financial instability can also impinge on a country's ability to pursue a prudent macroeconomic policy. The safety and soundness of financial institutions, therefore, have come to occupy a centre stage in the policy making.

CHAPTER V

MICRO LEVEL VARIABLES AND AGRICULTURAL CREDIT BY COMMERCIAL BANKS

5.1. Introduction

Agriculture and rural development are receiving increasing attention in The Third World Countries as a matter of sheer survival for a vast section of the rural population. India's population is predominantly rural in character with agriculture as the primary occupations. It was in this context the co-operative credit movement was started nearly 85 years ago as an institution to favour the agriculturists and release them from the clutches of informal lenders. But co-operatives seem to have failed to improve saving habits and improved lending services, both are important in rural development strategies. More stress should be given to inculcate saving habit among farmers to make them self-sustained.

The supply of farm credit generally has positive relation with the farm business income. The non-availability of farm credit affects the use of modern technology, fertilisers, pesticides, improved seeds, modern methods of cultivation etc., which in turn results in low productivity. The cheap and subsidized institutional credit facilities, to enhance their farm business income are needed. Supply leading finance can stimulate agricultural and rural development and contribute to target group productivity. Such assumptions motivated most of the low income countries to establish specialised farm credit to the targeted groups.

5.2. Agricultural Development and Subsidised Credit

Subsidised agricultural credit has been very popular in low-income countries on the usual assumption that such policies improve the welfare of small farmers. It is argued that small farmers are unable to borrow or will be able to borrow only in small amounts at high rates of interest unless they are aided by low-interest loans. Unfortunately the subsidy rarely reaches the poor. The amount of the subsidy is directly proportional to the size of the loan received. The larger the loan the larger the grant. In addition, since there is a high correlation between previous wealth and the size of the loan received, the weal their borrowers, the large are the grant. As a result, large producers have an access to large loans and to accompanying large grants. Medium size producers have access to small loans and to the associated small grants. Small producers get few or no loans and thus few or no grants. This is suggested that subsidised credit should be discouraged by the lending agencies.

Cheap and abundant credit is often regarded as an essential condition for agricultural development. This assumption has led donor agencies and governments to aggressively promote loans to farmers. But many studies in low-income counties revealed that the low interest rate policies are very closely associated with much of the poor performance of agricultural market. The main problems of cheap credit are loan concentration in the hands of relatively few borrowers, inefficient allocation of resources, high loan-transaction costs for some borrowers and lenders, politicization of financial institutions and weak financial intermediaries. The availability of cheap credit induces the farmers to take large agricultural loans for the namesake, but actually uses for other purposes or for re-lending, to get the benefit of reduced interest rate. It is clear that cheap credit undermines the agricultural development. Instead of providing cheap credit it is suggested that quick and timely credit should be made available to the farmers.

5.3. Interest Rate Regulation

Ceiling on interest rates and credit allocation (fixing and quotas) poses several problems in agricultural credit. In the process of interest ceiling, the government or its agency used to fix the lending rate as low as possible for the agricultural loans and lower interest rates on deposits mobilised by institutional agencies. It discourages deposit mobilisation on one hand and encourages more competition for farm credit on the other. In the process of credit rationing small farmers are forced to have limited access to institutional credit, while the rich farmers are allowed to enjoy lion's share of cheap credit. It also causes increased cost of credit to both borrower and lending agency. Any organisation or individual for that matter is beholded to those who provide support.

The banks or co-operatives that flow money from the central bank for lending to farmers, subject themselves to increased central bank control and the farmer who borrows is open to intrusions by the lender. Banks and agricultural service agencies may become addicted to the cheap funds provided by central banks especially, if they mobilise few local savings. This addiction makes these organisations vulnerable to political intrusions that may evolve into a virtual paternal relationship from top to bottom in the financial system.

In India, the state governments used to practice the co-operatives seem to be organized as department of state governments. The state governments for their political advantages used to give moratorium on farm credit, interest waiving etc., which affect the smooth functioning of the lending agencies, due to poor recovery, shortages of funds for re-lending, mounting overdue etc. This practice encourages the wilful defaulters, who hope that government may abolish the loan amount also. The financing agencies should improve their own resources for financing and over dependence on external agencies for funds should be minimised.

5.4. Bank Credit and Priority Sector Lending

Advances play an important role in the gross-earnings and net-profits of commercial banks and promote the economic development of the country. The basic function of credit whether provided by the banks or by other sources, is to enable individuals and business enterprises to purchase goods and services ahead of their ability or desire. Demand for credit arises because of the time consuming nature of the productive and distributive process. Consumer's demand, credit to acquire goods in advance for which they pay in future time. The gap between production, distribution and consumption, gives scope for the wide use of credit. According to the credit policy announced by the Reserve Bank of India in the second week of October, 1993, the banks have to allocate 40 percentage of bank credit to priority sector lending. If the commercial banks fail to achieve the stipulated level of priority-sector lending, the Reserve Bank of India would evoke the specified policies such as rising of reserve required to achieve the stipulated level of priority sectors lending.

According to the latest report of the Standing Committee of Finance of Tenth Lok Sabha, the real problem in priority sector lending is the lack of availability of timely credit. All efforts should be made to ensure timely availability of credit, by strengthening the resource position of the banks in rural areas. Agriculture was one of the sectors neglected by the commercial banks before nationalization of banks. The commercial banks were not willing to provide finance to agriculture in India. With the introduction of the social control measures, there came the realization on the commercial banks that it was no longer possible for them to keep away from such a crucial sector of the economy. They formulated various schemes to provide assistance to agriculture.

Gradually, with the introduction of the high-yielding varieties and increased uses of fertilizers, there was a shift from the subsistence nature of India farming to commercial farming and the surpluses were gradually increasing. With the development of other allied agricultural activities, the farmers were able to supplement their income from the crop production. This was, perhaps, one reason which created a new kind of confidence in the commercial banks that advances to agriculture would be as safe and productive as in any other sector. Commercial banks are providing directly and indirectly financial assistance to agricultural sector. In an indirect way, they are providing financial resources to agriculture through co-operative banks, land-mortgage banks and co-operative processing and market societies. Direct finance is extended for agricultural operations for short and medium periods to the farmers. The advances to agriculture have been increasing continuously. The proportion of agricultural advances in bank credit also increased.

5.5. Indebtedness of Farmer Households: Evidence from Tamil Nadu

Agriculture plays a key role in the overall economic and social well-being of our country. More than half of the workforce of the country are engaged in farming or allied activities. It is farmers who provide food and nutrition to the entire nation. They also provide livelihood to millions of people in the country. Over the years, India has moved from a state of food shortage to self-sufficiency in food, from importer of food grains to exporter of a variety of food items. Since the days of Green Revolution, our farmers have been using varieties of improved seeds and various sources of irrigation for their crops. On the other hand, a wide range of industrial inputs like fertilisers, pesticides and veterinary services for their livestock, are also being used by them. Many activities of farming have been mechanised and farmers are now accessing different dimensions of modern technology.[1]

Still it is not known how the farming communities in different regions of the country feel over the years; whether they are, at least, satisfied with their profession. To study the state of the Indian farmers, the Ministry of Agriculture planned a countrywide survey at the beginning of this millennium. The survey, known as 'Situation Assessment Survey of Farmers', was carried out on the basis of a sample of more than fifty thousand farmer households selected from all over the country. It was conducted by the National Sample Survey Organisation (NSSO) of its 59th round. Recently the 60th round of NSSO has begun from January 2013 and data collection will go up to December 2013.

Agriculture Minister Sharad Pawar told in the Parliament during September 2012 that according to the report, indebted farmers had a liability in cash or kind of Rs 300 or more at the time of the transaction. The number of indebted farmer households was highest in Andhra Pradesh 49.49 lakh or about 82 percentage of the estimated farm households in the state. Other states with high concentration were Tamil Nadu (74.5 percentage), Punjab (65.4 percentage), Kerala (64.4 percentage), Karnataka (61.6 percentage) and Maharashtra (54.8 percentage), the minister said.[2] This section discusses about the indebtedness of farmer households in TamilNadu.

---

[1]Report No. 498 (2005), *Situation Assessment Survey of Farmers Indebtedness of Farmer Households*: NSS 59th Round (January-December 2003).

[2]PTI (2011), The Farmer House holds in Debts, Agency, Newdelhi, September.

5.6. About the National Sample Survey

At the beginning of this century, the Union Ministry of Agriculture decided that a comprehensive survey to assess the situation of farmers in the country was necessary. The areas of interest included the educational level of farmer households; level of living as measured by consumer expenditure, income, productive assets and indebtedness; their farming practices and preferences;resource availability; awareness and access to technological developments etc. Accordingly, the Situation Assessment Survey of Farmers (SAS) was planned and conducted in 2003 by the National Sample Survey Organisation (NSSO) in the Ministry of Statistics & Programme Implementation. The survey was conducted only in the rural sector of the country. In all 51,770 households spread over 6,638 Blocks were surveyed in the central sample. The central sample covered the whole of the Indian Union except (i) Leh (Ladakh) and Kargil districts of Jammu & Kashmir, (ii) interior Blocks of Nagaland situated beyond five kilometers of any bus route and (iii) Blocks in Andaman and Nicobar Islands which remain inaccessible throughout the year.

All the technical work relating to this survey including, among others, development of sampling design, survey methodology and preparation of the report was undertaken by the Survey Design and Research Division of NSSO. The field work for the survey was handled by the Field Operations Division. The collected data were processed by the Data Processing Division. The overall co-ordination among different divisions was done by the Coordination and Publication Division. [1]

To look closely at the problem of indebtedness of the farmers to the money lenders, and their lack of access to institutional credit, the Ministry of agriculture (GOI) constituted a Task force on 6th October 2009. The task force visited 45 Blocks across 17 states including Tamil Nadu (Kanchipuram and Sivaganga) and held state level consultations, to understand from men and women farmers what the issues were and what now needs to be done to ensure that smallest of farmers can access at reasonable rates and reasonable terms. This task force report also properly evidenced at the necessary place. [2]

---

[1]Ray (2005), "Report No. 498: Situation Assessment Survey of Farmers Indebtedness of Farmer Households: NSS 59th Round.

[2]GOI (2010), Ministry of Agriculture, *Report of the Task Force on Credit Related Issues of Farmers*, June, p.28

Table 5.1: Numbers of Blocks Allotted and Surveyed and Number of Farmer Households and Persons Surveyed in Tamil Nadu

Particulars	No. of Blocks		No. of sample farmer Households	No. of sample persons
	Allotted	Surveyed		
All India	6760	6638	51770	286503
Tamil Nadu	412	404	3189	13870
% Share of Tamil Nadu	6.09	6.086	6.16	4.841

Source: Situation Assessment Survey of Farmers Indebtedness of Farmer Households: NSS 59th Round (January–December 2003).

From the above table, it is observed that the sample share of Tamil Nadu out of the central sample which includes the entire nation represents around more than 6 % of different categories of farmers. It is clear from the table that that the number of sample persons shows only around 4% out of the central sample.

Table 5.2: Estimated Number of Rural Households and Total and Indebted Farmer Households in Tamil Nadu

Particulars	Estimated Number of RH ('00)	Estimated Number of FH ('00)	Estimated Number of IDFH ('00)	Percentage of FH Indebted
All India	1478988	893504	434242	48.6
Tamil Nadu	110182	38880	28954	74.5
Share of Tamil Nadu in %	7.45	4.35	6.66	x

RH: Rural Households; FH: Farmer Households; IDFH: Indebted Farmer Households

Source: Situation Assessment Survey of Farmers Indebtedness of Farmer Households: NSS 59th Round (January–December 2003).

From the table 5.2, it is evident that the sample share of Tamil Nadu out of the central sample at all-India level, an estimated 60.4% of rural households are farmer households and of them 48.6% are reported to be indebted. The incidence of indebtedness is the highest in Andhra Pradesh (82.0%), followed by Tamil Nadu (74.5%). States with very low proportion of indebted farmer households are Meghalaya, Arunachal Pradesh and Uttaranchal. In each of these States less than 10% farmer households are indebted.[1]

[1]Situation Assessment Survey of Farmers Indebtedness of Farmer Households: NSS 59th Round.

Table 5.3: Distribution of All Farmer Households by Social Group in Tamil Nadu

Particulars	ST	SC	OBC	Others	All	Estimated No. of FH	Sample No. of FH
All India	133	175	415	276	1000	893504	51770
Tamil Nadu	43	211	733	13	1000	38880	3189
Share of Tamil Nadu	32.3	120.6	176.67	4.71	100	4.35	6.16
Estimated No. of Hhs '00	119241	155926	370430	246884	893504	x	x
Sample No. of Hhs '00	7996	9089	20019	14585	51770	x	x

Source: Situation Assessment Survey of Farmers Indebtedness of Farmer Households: NSS 59th Round (January–December 2003). RH: Rural Households; FH: Farmer Households; IDFH: Indebted Farmer Households

The table 5.3 reveals that the percentage share of estimated all farmer households in different social groups are 13.3% in ST, 17.5% in SC, 41.5% in OBC and 27.7% in others. At Tamil Nadu level, 4.3% farmer households are from ST, 21.1 % of households are from SC group and 73.3 % of people are from OBC which constitutes majority of the population.

Table 5.4: Distribution of All indebted Farmer Households by Social Group in Tamil Nadu

Particulars	ST	SC	OBC	Others	All	Estimated No. of FH	Sample No. of FH
All India	100	180	439	281	1000	434242	23935
Tamil Nadu	42	219	729	10	1000	28954	2254
Share of Tamil Nadu	42	121.6	166	3.55	100	6.66	9.42
Estimated No. of Hhs '00	119241	155926	370430	246884	893504	x	x
Estimated No. of IDH	43304	78323	190467	122014	434242	x	x
Sample No. of Hhs '00	7996	9089	20019	14585	51770	x	x

Source: Situation Assessment Survey of Farmers Indebtedness of Farmer Households: NSS 59th Round (January- December 2003). RH: Rural Households; FH: Farmer Households; IDFH: Indebted Farmer Households

The table 5.4 shows that the percentage share of estimated all farmer households in different social groups are 13.3% in ST, 17.5% in SC, 41.5% in OBC and 27.7% in Others. At all India level, 48.6% farmer households were indebted. The prevalence rates of indebtedness of farmer households in different social groups was 36.3% in ST, 50.2% in SC, 51.4% in OBC and 49.4% in others. Thus, excluding farmer households belonging to ST, around half of the households in all other social groups were indebted. Among 100 indebted farmer households, it is observed that 10 households belong to ST, 18 households to SC, 44 households to OBC and 28 households to others. Between the two states, namely, Andhra Pradesh[1] and Tamil Nadu where, as already mentioned, a vast majority of farming community was indebted. It is observed that in Andhra Pradesh 11% belong to ST, 17% to SC, 47% to OBC and 25% to Others, whereas the percentages are 4%, 22%, 73% and 1% respectively in Tamil Nadu.

[1]Situation Assessment Survey of Farmers Indebtedness of Farmer Households: NSS 59th Round.

Table 5.5: Distribution of Farmer Households by Source of Income in Tamil Nadu

Particulars	Cultivation	Farming other than Cultivation	Other Agricultural Activity	Others	All	Estimated No. of FH	Sample No. of FH
All India	572	30	39	359	1000	893504	51770
Tamil Nadu	490	65	41	404	1000	38880	3189
Share of Tamil Nadu	85.67	216.67	105.12	112.53	100	4.35	6.16
Estimated No. of Hhs '00	119241	155926	370430	246884	893504	x	x
Estimated No. of IDH	43304	78323	190467	122014	434242	x	x
Sample No. of Hhs '00	7996	9089	20019	14585	51770	x	x

RH: Rural Households; FH: Farmer Households; IDFH: Indebted Farmer Households ; Source: Situation Assessment Survey of Farmers Indebtedness of Farmer Households: NSS 59th Round (January–December 2003).

The table 5.5 reveals per thousand distribution of total farmer Households by source of income in Tamil Nadu and it shows per thousand distribution of indebted farmer households by different sources of income. The principal source of income of farmer households are categorised as cultivation, farming other than cultivation, other agricultural activities, and others. Here, 'cultivation' means activities related to production of crops by tillage and related ancillary activities. 'Farming other than cultivation' includes animal husbandry, poultry, fishery, piggery, bee-keeping etc.; whereas growing of trees, horticultural crops (orchards) and plantations (rubber, cashew, pepper, coffee, tea, etc.) are considered under 'other agricultural activity'. And 'other' comprises wage/salaried employment, non-agricultural enterprises, pension, remittances, interest and dividends, and other sources. [1]

Table 5.6: Distribution of Indebted Farmer Households by Source of Income in Tamil Nadu

Particulars	Cultivation	Farming other than Cultivation	Other Agricultural Activity	Others	All	Estimated No.of FH	Sample No.of FH
All India	569	32	41	357	1000	434242	23935
Tamil Nadu	507	57	31	405	1000	28954	2254
Share of Tamil Nadu	89.10	178.12	75.60	113.45	100	6.66	9.42
Estimated No. of Hhs '00	119241	155926	370430	246884	893504	x	x
Estimated No. of IDH	43304	78323	190467	122014	434242	x	x
Sample No. of Hhs '00	7996	9089	20019	14585	51770	x	x

RH: Rural Households; FH: Farmer Households; IDFH: Indebted Farmer Households ; Source: Situation Assessment Survey of Farmers Indebtedness of Farmer Households: NSS 59th Round (January–December 2003).

[1]Situation Assessment Survey of Farmers Indebtedness of Farmer Households: NSS 59th Round.

The table 5.5 and 5.6 reveals that out of the total number of farmer households an estimated 57.2% are 'cultivators' and among these 48.4% are indebted. 3.0% farmer households have source of income' farming other than cultivation', 3.9% have 'other agricultural activities' and 35.9% have 'others', and in each of these categories about 48-52% households were indebted. On an average, out of 100 indebted farmer households, 56.9 % households have cultivation as source of income. 3.2% have 'farming other than cultivation', and 4.1% have 'other agricultural activities' and 35.7% have 'others'. In Tamil Nadu level, 49.0% are 'cultivators' and among these 48.4% are indebted. 6.5% farmer households have farming other than cultivation', 4.1% have 'other agricultural activities' and 40.4% have 'others', are indebted. On an average, out of 100 indebted farmer households, 50.7% households have cultivation, 5.7% have 'farming other than cultivation', and 3.1 have 'other agricultural activities' and 40.5% have others.

Table 5.7: Distribution of Outstanding Loans (in Rs.) by Different Sources of Income of ST Farmer Households in Tamil Nadu

Source of income	*a*	*b*	*c*	*d*	*e*	*f*	*g*	*h*	*i*	*j*	*k*	*l*
Cultivation	299	380	0	39	67	0	0	216	1000	734	950	50
Farming other Than cultivation	13	15	0	32	98	0	0	842	1000	770	114	9
Other agricultural Activity	0	273	0	109	16	0	0	602	1000	992	96	9
Others	638	28	3	74	90	39	94	32	1000	654	500	48
All	351	278	1	50	71	9	22	219	1000	728	1661	116
Estd. No. farmer Hhs (00)	230	470	9	307	95	16	4	147	1208	x	x	x
Sample No. of farmer Hhs	3	27	2	25	10	2	1	8	80	x	x	x

a.Capital expenditure in farm business; **b.**Current expenditure in farm business; **c.**Non-farm business; **d.**Consumption expenditure; **e.**Marriages and ceremonies; **f.**Education medical treatment; **g.**Medical treatment; **h.**Other expenditure; **i.**All; **j.**All No.Per 1000 of indebted Hhs; **k.**Estimated No.of farmer Hhs (00); **l.**Sample No.of farmer Hhs

Source: Situation Assessment Survey of Farmers Indebtedness of Farmer Households: NSS 59th Round (January–December 2003)

The table 5.7 clearly shows the source of income of farmers and how they spend on different purposes and how they give priority in meeting the expenditure requirement. From the cultivation source of income 38% of the income reaches in meeting the current expenditure in farm business and 30% of the people invest their money in building infrastructure for the farm development. Majority of the income (84.2%) from farming other than cultivation is spent on other categories instead of agriculture. Another interesting fact that is other sources of income are also highly diverted to (63.8%) agriculture. These results are confined to Scheduled Tribes Groups in Tamil Nadu.

Table 5.8: Distribution of Outstanding Loans (in Rs.) by Different Sources of Income of SC Farmer Households in Tamil Nadu

Source of income	*a*	*b*	*c*	*d*	*e*	*f*	*g*	*h*	*i*	*j*	*k*	*l*
Cultivation	179	275	10	73	89	51	5	317	1000	846	2995	182
Farming other Than cultivation	750	50	0	122	53	6	12	7	1000	636	445	73
Other agricultural Activity	51	388	4	297	57	135	60	8	1000	787	313	46
Others	264	61	7	255	169	54	48	142	1000	738	4451	443
All	237	170	8	164	124	53	26	218	1000	774	8204	744
Estd. No.farmer Hhs (00)	1129	1806	191	2800	879	257	317	563	6346	X	X	X
Sample No.Of farmer Hhs	75	129	10	255	70	15	36	39	537	X	X	X

a.Capital expenditure in farm business; **b.**Current expenditure in farm business; **c.**Non-farm business; **d.**Consumption expenditure; **e.**Marriages and ceremonies; **f.**Education medical treatment; **g.**Medical treatment; **h.**Other expenditure; **i.**All;**j.**All No. Per 1000 of indebted Hhs; **k.**Estimated No.of farmer Hhs (00); **l.**Sample No.of farmer Hhs

Source: Situation Assessment Survey of Farmers Indebtedness of Farmer Households: NSS 59th Round (January–December 2003)

From the above table 5.8, it is observed that out of the total number of farmer households belonging to scheduled caste and their source of income, only 27.5% farmer households have cultivation and spend their money in capital expenditure for farm business. 75% farmer households have farming other than cultivation focus on capital expenditure to the farm land. 38.8% have 'other agricultural activities' and spend money related to farm business. 16.9% of farmers come under 'others' categories spend considerable amount in marriages and ceremonies.

Table 5.9: Distribution of Outstanding Loans (in Rs.) by Different Sources of Income of OBC Farmer Households in Tamil Nadu

Source of income	*a*	*b*	*c*	*d*	*e*	*f*	*g*	*h*	*i*	*j*	*k*	*l*
Cultivation	318	336	24	74	96	19	18	115	1000	763	14831	887
Farming other Than cultivation	73	212	78	231	44	17	166	179	1000	648	1934	210
Other agricultural Activity	199	420	76	189	11	38	29	38	1000	483	1169	131
Others	119	133	129	213	67	29	78	233	1000	754	10564	1045
All	235	260	65	132	82	23	45	158	1000	740	28498	2273
Estd. No.farmer Hhs (00)	4255	8569	909	6593	1762	718	1707	2664	21095	X	X	X
Sample No.of farmer Hhs	316	519	87	565	148	47	117	198	1602	X	X	X

a.Capital expenditure in farm business; **b.**Current expenditure in farm business; **c.**Non-farm business; **d.**Consumption expenditure; **e.**Marriages and ceremonies; **f.**Education medical treatment; **g.**Medical treatment; **h.**Other expenditure; **i.**All; **j.**All No.Per 1000 of indebted Hhs; **k.**Estimated No.of farmer Hhs (00); **l.**Sample No.of farmer Hhs

Source: Situation Assessment Survey of Farmers Indebtedness of Farmer Households: NSS 59th Round (January–December 2003)

The table 5.9 reveals the per thousand distributions of total farmer households by source of income in Tamil Nadu by social group on other backward class. The principal source of income of farmer households is categorised as cultivation, 33.6% of the income is only to meet out the current expenditure in farm business. 21.2% of income from farming other than agricultural cultivation are spent in meeting the capital expenditure in farm business.

Table 5.10: Distribution of Outstanding Loans (in Rs.) by Different Sources of Income of Others Farmer Households in Tamil Nadu

Source of income	*a*	*b*	*c*	*d*	*e*	*f*	*g*	*h*	*i*	*j*	*k*	*l*
Cultivation	563	256	0	8	166	7	0	0	1000	489	293	25
Farming other Than cultivation	0	842	0	158	0	0	0	0	1000	810	26	5
Other agricultural Activity	0	0	0	0	0	0	0	0	0	0	3	2
Others	178	425	0	94	6	7	0	291	1000	715	195	24
All	469	300	0	29	128	7	0	66	1000	587	517	56
Estd. No.farmer Hhs (00)	78	192	0	47	6	12	0	15	304	x	x	x
Sample No.Of farmer Hhs	10	15	0	12	2	2	0	3	35	x	x	x

a.Capital expenditure in farm business; **b**.Current expenditure in farm business; **c**.Non-farm business; **d**.Consumption expenditure; **e**.Marriages and ceremonies; **f**.Education medical treatment; **g**.Medical treatment; **h**.Other expenditure; **i**.All; **j**.All No.Per 1000 of indebted Hhs; **k**.Estimated No.of farmer Hhs (00); **l**.Sample No.of farmer Hhs

Source: Situation Assessment Survey of Farmers Indebtedness of Farmer Households: NSS 59th Round (January–December 2003)

The table 5.10 discloses the per thousand distributions of total farmer households by source of income in Tamil Nadu and per thousand distributions of indebted farmer households by different sources of income for the social group under 'others'. 56.3% of the income is spent in meeting the capital expenditure in farm business. The interesting fact is that 84.2% of the income from farming other than cultivation activity is spent on the current expenditure in farm business.

Table 5.11: Distribution of Outstanding Loans (in Rs.) by Different Sources of Income of All Farmer Households in Tamil Nadu

Source of income	*a*	*b*	*c*	*d*	*e*	*f*	*g*	*h*	*i*	*j*	*k*	*l*
Cultivation	309	331	21	71	95	21	15	136	1000	770	19069	1144
Farming other Than cultivation	152	186	65	209	47	15	139	188	1000	653	2520	297
Other agricultural Activity	162	403	59	196	17	48	37	78	1000	573	1581	188
Others	152	123	108	214	82	33	73	216	1000	746	15710	1560
All	243	251	55	131	87	26	41	166	1000	745	38880	3189
Estd. No.farmer Hhs (00)	5692	11037	1109	9746	2742	1003	2029	3389	28954	x	x	x
Sample No.of farmer Hhs	414	690	99	857	230	66	154	248	2254	x	x	x

a.Capital expenditure in farm business; **b**.Current expenditure in farm business; **c**.Non-farm business; **d**.Consumption expenditure; **e**.Marriages and ceremonies; **f**.Education medical treatment; **g**.Medical treatment; **h**.Other expenditure; **i**.All; **j**.All No.Per 1000 of indebted Hhs; **k**.Estimated No.of farmer Hhs (00); **l**.Sample No.of farmer Hhs

Source: Situation Assessment Survey of Farmers Indebtedness of Farmer Households: NSS 59th Round (January–December 2003)

The table 5.11 clearly illustrates the sources of income of farmers of different social groups of Tamil Nadu, how they spend on different purposes and how they give priority in meeting the expenditure requirements. From the cultivation source of income 30.9% of the income reaches in meeting the capital expenditure in farm business. 33.1% of the people invest their money in building infrastructure and considerable share is allotted to social functions like marriage and ceremonies. 20.9 % of the of income from farming other than cultivation is spent on consumption expenditure. From the overall data, it is clear that the current expenditure on farm activity alone contributes one fourth (25.1) of the total farming community.

Table 5.12: Distribution of Outstanding Loans (in Rs.) by Each Size Class of Land Possessed by Farmer Households in Tamil Nadu

Size class of Land Possesed (ha)	*a*	*b*	*c*	*d*	*e*	*f*	*g*	*h*	*i*	*j*	*k*	*l*
< 0.01 (A)	149	89	26	444	119	15	76	82	1000	600	913	353
0.01 - 0.40(B)	137	89	151	214	136	47	54	172	1000	704	13642	1292
0.40 - 1.00(C)	159	264	36	159	78	22	60	223	1000	787	13990	829
1.01 - 2.00(D)	308	277	13	88	120	10	42	142	1000	787	5672	437
2.01 - 4.00(E)	352	376	17	70	59	7	15	103	1000	738	3650	211
4.01 -10.00(F)	440	302	12	53	13	58	0	122	1000	604	1035	59
10.00+ (G)	277	186	429	0	0	0	0	109	1000	785	158	8
All Sizes (H)	243	251	55	131	87	26	41	166	1000	745	38880	3189
Estd. No.of farmer Hhs (00)	5692	11037	1109	9746	2742	1003	2029	3389	28954	x	x	x
Sample No.of farmer Hhs	414	690	99	857	230	66	154	248	2254	x	x	x

a.Capital expenditure in farm business; **b.**Current expenditure in farm business; **c.**Non-farm business; Consumption expenditure; **e.**Marriages and ceremonies; **f.**Education medical treatment; **g.**Medical treatment; **h.**Other expenditure; **i.**All; **j.**All No.Per 1000 of indebted Hhs; **k.**Estimated No.of farmer Hhs (00); **l.**Sample No.of farmer Hhs

Source: Situation Assessment Survey of Farmers Indebtedness of Farmer Households: NSS 59th Round (January–December 2003)

The table 5.12, shows the percentage share of expenses with different their land class holdings. This table is related to Tamil Nadu based on farmer households with size of land possessed. From the land size class (A), it is observed that maximum has gone only to consumption purpose and minimum is spent on education and medical treatment. These land size classes prefer to spend only in marriages and ceremonies. The land size class (C) focuses on other expenditure and land class (D) focuses on capital expenditure in farm business. From the above table, it is clear that land size class E, F, and G focus on capital expenditure in farm business. The overall (H) class of farmers give preference to spend their money in current expenditure in farm business.

Table 5.13: Distribution of Outstanding Loans (in Rs.) by Each Size Class of Land Possessed by Farmer Households in India

Size class of Land Possesed	*a*	*b*	*c*	*d*	*e*	*f*	*g*	*h*	*i*	*j*	*k*	*l*
< 0.01 (A)	151	57	77	212	224	3	130	147	1000	453	12594	2598
0.01 - 0.40 (B)	133	95	123	146	201	10	72	220	1000	444	292867	19116
0.40 - 1.00 (C)	241	227	103	105	133	13	41	137	1000	456	283610	13373
1.01 - 2.00 (D)	326	320	46	87	99	5	24	93	1000	510	160600	8627
2.01 - 4.00 (E)	388	347	47	50	89	7	13	59	1000	582	93504	4973
4.01 -10.00 (F)	411	398	23	59	50	5	12	41	1000	651	42581	2696
10.00+ (G)	457	325	32	48	29	15	37	57	1000	664	7748	387
All Sizes (H)	306	278	67	88	111	8	33	108	1000	486	893504	51770
Estd. No.of farmer Hhs (00)	105262	158564	22222	101526	49556	3951	28467	45596	434242	x	x	x
Sample No.of farmer Hhs	5453	7432	1598	6300	2666	275	1597	3001	23935	x	x	x

a.Capital expenditure in farm business; **b.**Current expenditure in farm business; **c.**Non-farm business; **d.** Consumption expenditure; **e.**Marriages and ceremonies; **f.**Education; **g.**Medical treatment; **h.**Other expenditure; **i.** All; **j.** All No.Per 1000 of indebted Hhs; **k.** Estimated No.of farmer Hhs (00); **l.** Sample No. of farmer Hhs

Source: Situation Assessment Survey of Farmers Indebtedness of Farmer Households: NSS 59th Round (January–December 2003)

The table 5.13, it reveals the percentage share of expenses with different land class holdings and the loan amount. This table is confined to all India which includes all the states of country, based on farmer household in each size class of land possessed. From the land size class (A), it is interpreted high amount is spent on marriages and ceremonies which are considered as indispensible social activities. A small amount is spent on education. The land size classes are (C), (D), (E), (F), (G) and (H) focus on capital and current expenditure in farm business.

Table 5.14: Distribution of Outstanding Loans (in Rs.) by Source of Loan for Each Size Class of Land Possessed by Farmer Households in Tamil Nadu

Size class of Land Possesed	*a*	*b*	*c*	*d*	*e*	*f*	*g*	*h*	*i*	*j*	*k*
< 0.01(A)	5	107	79	689	19	74	0	27	1000	548	214
0.01 - 0.40 (B)	15	181	178	509	5	97	0	14	1000	9483	874
0.40 - 1.00 (C)	21	235	204	494	3	32	1	10	1000	11014	627
1.01 - 2.00 (D)	19	235	361	299	4	72	3	8	1000	4466	328
2.01 - 4.00 (E)	37	325	290	286	8	47	0	6	1000	2695	161
4.01 -10.00 (F)	3	212	528	244	3	6	2	2	1000	625	44
10.00+ (G)	0	114	715	63	0	0	0	109	1000	124	6
All Sizes (H)	20	233	281	397	4	52	1	11	1000	28954	2254
Estd. No.of farmer Hhs '00	992	9448	6768	15050	518	3077	44	620	28954	x	x
sample No.of farmer Hhs '00	74	667	482	1165	58	261	7	74	2254	x	x

a. Government; **b**. Cooperative; **c**.Bank; **d**.Agricultural/professional money lender; **e**.Trader **f**. Relatives and friends **g**. Doctors, Lawyers and other Professionals; **h**.Others ; **i**.All; **J**.Estimated; **K**.Sample

Source: Situation Assessment Survey of Farmers Indebtedness of Farmer Households: NSS 59th Round (January-December 2003)

The above table 5.14, clearly shows the source of loan agencies including the banks. It is apparent from the table that majority of the farmers in Tamil Nadu are depending on Block/Agricultural professional money lenders for their financial requirement irrespective of the different land class holdings. In the land size class (A), it is observed that higher numbers of farmers are depending on Block money lenders for their financial requirements. Majority of the land size class (B) and (C) are also depending on money lenders for their financial requirement. From the table, it is evident that the persons belonging to (B) and (C) class categories, are also utilising cooperative and commercial banks for the financial need which are more or less equal to the numbers of people who are in the clutches of money lenders.

As the land size class increases from (C) to (G), the farmers start shifting from the money lenders to the formal financial institutions i.e. cooperatives and commercial banks. It is clear from the above, that out of thousand farmers 39.7% rely on Block professional money lenders for their credit need in farm business. The overall (H) class of farmers give preference (around 50% of the farmers) borrow from only the formal financial institutions which is comparatively equal to the national average. This finding is also substantiated by the fact that, the share of cooperatives in the total outstanding debt of farmers is only 19.6%. However, in the five states of Gujarat, Haryana Kerala, Maharashtra and Tamil Nadu, cooperative credit societies are an important source of credit (shares being in the range of 23-49%). However, in some cases the credit lines are choked, they could be reflecting old rather than current year loans.[1]

Table 5.15: Distribution of Outstanding Loans (in Rs.) by Source of Loan for Each Size Class of Land Possessed by Farmer Households in India

Size class of Land Possesed	*a*	*b*	*c*	*D*	*e*	*f*	*g*	*h*	*i*	*j*	*k*
< 0.01	19	53	154	473	40	231	10	20	1000	5708	1220
0.01 - 0.40	40	145	248	318	49	149	14	37	1000	130112	8538
0.40 - 1.00	38	170	320	308	46	91	7	20	1000	129211	5702
1.01 - 2.00	17	205	354	259	42	88	8	26	1000	81920	3906
2.01 - 4.00	15	226	410	234	47	51	4	14	1000	54409	2676
4.01 -10.00	13	230	445	167	61	56	15	12	1000	27734	1633
10.00+	17	232	427	172	106	40	0	6	1000	5148	260
All Sizes	25	196	356	257	52	85	9	21	1000	434242	23935
Estd. No.of farmer Hhs (00)	14769	114785	117100	125000	53902	77602	7181	14605	434242	x	x
sample No.of farmer Hhs	992	5844	6296	6919	3018	4528	345	872	23935	x	x

a.Government; **b.**Cooperative; **c.**Bank; **d.**Agricultural/professional money lender; **e.**Trader; **f.** Relatives and friends; **g.** Doctors, Lawyers and other Professionals; **h.**Others ; **i.**All; **J.**Estimated; **K.**Sample

Source: Situation Assessment Survey of Farmers Indebtedness of Farmer Households: NSS 59th Round (January–December 2003).

From the table 5.15 it is clear that the share of non-institutional agencies in the debt and incidence of indebtedness decreased with the size of land holding. The share of non institutional agencies in the debt is 77% for the near landless (less than 0.01 hectares), 57% for the sub-marginal farmers (0.01-0.40 hectares), 47% for the upper marginal farmers (0.4-1.0 hectares), 42% for small farmers (1-2 hectares) and stood at a reduced, yet significant, 32% for large farmers (10 hectares and above). Though 80% of indebted farmer households are those from among small and marginal farmers, institutional agencies account for only half of their debt. Thus, as far as access to formal credit is concerned, small and marginal farmer households are at a disadvantage. Even large farmers take recourse to informal sources though they are better served by institutional agencies.[2] The above said estimate is pertained to all India level by the task force but this is also consistent with the data provided by National Sample Survey on indebtedness of farmers.

[1]GOI (2010), Ministry of Agriculture, *Report of the Task Force on Credit Related Issues of Farmers*, June, pp.28.

[2]ibid, 29.

More than three-fifths of the outstanding debt (formal plus informal) of cultivators in 2002 was for productive purposes. It increased from 40% in 1961 to 72% in 1981 and then showed a decline to 63% in 2002. At the all India level the total debt of farmer households was estimated at Rs.1,12,000 crore in 2003. Of the total debt, Rs.48,000 crore was sourced from non-institutional agencies, of which Rs.18,000 crore of debt carried an interest rate greater than 30%. As already mentioned, in agriculture, where the returns are much lower, this is a matter of serious concern.[1]

5.7. Institutional Credit for Agriculture at Block Level

Institutional credit to agricultural farmers at District and Block levels is the key restraint due to the decentralized system. It is required to make certain that concerns of farmers be mainstreamed into the area growth approach to the origin levels. Conventional approaches to development have miserably failed to reflect the concerns and priorities of the farmers. Even though the provisions of Central Planning Commission are necessitated to bring farmers into the local governance, yet they are inadequate to address the concerns and priorities of them.

Very importantly needed are the tools and mechanisms that can integrate farmers in the process of planning and development. Mainstreaming credit process at the District and Block levels is an effective means of enabling integration of farmer's concerns and priority resulting in equitable development. This would guarantee the institutional credit in district plan and through allocations made in the District Budgets.

Too much emphasis on targets rather on actual needs of credit is one of the major problems. It is common now in India to organise credit fairs for mass distribution of agricultural credit to achieve target lending. In the process of mass distribution of credit, proper evaluation of credit worthiness of the borrower and feasibility of the credit proposal is not possible. It results in poor recovery to the lender. Alone with the credit fairs, the credit recovery should also be organised effectively by the lending agencies to get fruitful result.

5.8. Profile of the Study Area

Gobichettipalayam Block

Gobichettipalayam Block is very wealthy in agriculture with a total area of 23,058 hectares with a population of 68,659 and having 5 Town Panchayats, 20 Block Panchayats. The block has 17,272 hectares of irrigated lands and an extent of 1,972 hectares of land is fallow/cultivable waste.

[1]ibid, 48.

These wastelands could be brought under plantation/Horticulture and agro-forestry crops like Mango, Guava, Teak, Tamarind, Silk, Cotton, Sapota etc.

The Block has vast scope for development of Poultry farming, Sericulture, Fish farming in constructed ponds, stall-fed goat rearing under Agriculture allied activities. Mushroom activity is picking up in the block for the last 2 years. The Block also offers scope for establishing agro-based industries, Handloom and Power loom based units. Rural industries may be supported through KVIC scheme and very good exploitable potentials are identified in the block. Self Help Group formation is fast picking up in this area and the groups may be motivated to take up non-traditional viable agricultural and industrial activities.

Anthiyur Block

Next to agriculture, powerlooms occupy an important place in the economy of the block. Forests occupy about 80,570 hectares of land in the block. The important forest products are sandalwood, rosewood, timber, firewood, tamarind, honey etc., The block offers good potential for the development of sericulture, poultry farming, stall-fed-goat rearing, fish culture in constructed ponds, sweet orange, citrus etc., Fallow lands constitute about 3,270 hectres which can be brought under horticulture and agro forestry crops like mango, guava, sweet orange, citrus, cashew, sapota, casuarina, eucalyptus, teak, silk cotton etc. Paddy is being cultivated in 970 hectres of land. Kambu and Ragi are the major products that are being cultivated in the block.

The main aim of this section is to inspect the formal credit for the agricultural sector of the two Blocks of Erode district in Tamil Nadu. The proportional study between the two Blocks of Erode district was selected where the area of operation of SBI, Gobichettipalayam branch and SBI Anthiyur branch, and who have exclusively borrowed from the SBI to understand and review institutional credit at Block level.

The overall purpose of the work is to examine the variations in the institutional credit flow to farmers at Block level. The farmers with less than 3 acres of operational holding are considered as Marginal Farmers. The farmers with 4 to 8 acres of operational holding are considered as Small Farmers and the farmers possessed with more than 8 acres of operational holding are lying in the category of large farmers. The low level age group lies to the extreme level of 30. The middle level of age group is between 30-50. The age after 50 is considered as high age group.

Table 5.16: Age Level of Sample Households

Block - Gobichettipalayam (1)				
Particulars	**Low**	**Middle**	**High**	**Total**
Marginal Farmers	14 *(16.5)*	47 *(55.3)*	24*(28.5)*	85 *(100)*
Small Farmers	10 *(8.5)*	64 *(54.7)*	43 *(36.8)*	117 *(100)*
Large Farmers	8 *(16.7)*	19 *(39.5)*	21*(43.7)*	48 *(100)*
Total	32 *(12.8)*	130 *(52)*	88 *(35.2)*	250 *(100)*
Block - Anthiyur (2)				
Marginal Farmers	11*(13.4)*	54*(65.8)*	17 *(20.7)*	82 *(100)*
Small Farmers	33 *(25.2)*	72 *(55)*	26 *(19.8)*	131*(100)*
Large Farmers	7 *(19)*	16 *(43.2)*	14 *(37.8)*	37 *(100)*
Total	51*(20.4)*	142 *(56.8)*	57 *(22.8)*	250 *(100)*

Source: Field Data

The total population of Block -1, from the sample is 250. Out of the total 250 respondents, 32 belong to Low age group; 130 people belong to the middle age group, 88 people are in High age group. In, Block-2 it has a total population of 250 persons out of whom 51 are said to be in Low age group; 142 are under the category of middle age group, 57 are in the high age group. Table-5.16, shown the age level of 250 households are belonging to the two sample Blocks. It is found that, middle age group in Block-I is 53.2 percentage and 56.8 percentage in Block-II.

Table 5.17: Gender of Sample Households

Block - Gobichettipalayam (1)			
Particulars	**Male**	**Female**	**Total**
Marginal Farmers	73*(85.8)*	12 *(14.2)*	85*(100)*
Small Farmers	98 *(83.8)*	19 *(16.2)*	117*(100)*
Large Farmers	42 *(87.5)*	6 *(12.5)*	48 *(100)*
Total	213*(85.2)*	37 *(14.8)*	250 *(100)*
Block - Anthiyur (2)			
Marginal Farmers	69 *(84.2)*	13 *(15.8)*	82 *(100)*
Small Farmers	112 *(85.5)*	19 *(14.5)*	131*(100)*
Large Farmers	31*(83.8)*	6 *(16.2)*	37 *(100)*
Total	212 *(84.8)*	38 *(15.2)*	250 *(100)*

Source: Field Data

The sample population of Block-1 is 250. Out of the total 250 persons, 213 are Male and 37 are Female. It is clear from the table that, majority of them are small farmers. In Block-2, out of 250 persons 212 are Male and 38 are Female. Table-5.17, shows the Gender of 250 households belonging to the two sample Blocks. It is found that 84.2 percentage are Male in Block-I and 84.3 percentage are female in Block-II. Table 5.18, shows the of Size of 500 households belonging to the two sample Blocks. It is clear that Medium size family category in Block-1 consists of 49.2 percentage and 56 percentage in Block-2.

Table 5.18: Size of the Family of Sample Households

Block - Gobichettipalayam (1)				
Particulars	**Small**	**Medium**	**Large**	**Total**
Marginal Farmers	23 *(27.1)*	37 *(43.5)*	25 *(29.4)*	85 *(100)*
Small Farmers	10 *(8.5)*	64 *(54.7)*	43 *(36.8)*	117 *(100)*
Large Farmers	14 *(29.2)*	22 *(45.8)*	12 *(25.0)*	48 *(100)*
Total	47 *(18.8)*	123 *(49.2)*	80 *(32.0)*	250 *(100)*
Block - Anthiyur (2)				
Marginal Farmers	21 *(25.6)*	44 *(53.7)*	17 *(20.7)*	82 *(100)*
Small Farmers	25 *(19.1)*	82 *(62.6)*	24 *(18.3)*	131*(100)*
Large Farmers	9 *(24.4)*	21 *(56.7)*	7 *(18.9)*	37 *(100)*
Total	53 *(21.2)*	140 *(56.0)*	57 *(22.8)*	250 *(100)*

Source: Field Data

For the purpose of the study, the family which has members up to 3 is considered as small. Members from 3 to 5 is considered as Medium and the has more than 5 members is considered as large. Out of the total 250 persons from Block 1, 47 are from small family, 123 are from Medium size family and 80 are from Large family. Out of 250 persons from Block 2, 53 are from small family, 140 are from Medium size family and 57 are from Large family size.

Table 5.19, shows the level of education of 500 households belonging to the two sample Blocks are shown. Overall the proportions of literates in Block-1 consist of about 35 percentage against 40 percentage in Block-2.

Table 5.19: Literacy and Education of Sample Households

Block - Gobichettipalayam (1)						
Particulars	**Illiterates**	**up to 5th**	**up to 10th**	**up to HSC**	**Above HSC**	**Total**
Marginal Farmers	38 *(44.7)*	17 *(20.0)*	11 *(12.9)*	10 *(10.8)*	9 *(10.6)*	85 *(100)*
Small Farmers	48 *(41.0)*	30 *(25.6)*	18 *(15.4)*	14 *(12.0)*	7 *(6.0)*	117 *(100)*
Large Farmers	18 *(37.4)*	10 *(20.8)*	3 *(6.2)*	9 *(18.7)*	8 *(16.7)*	48 *(100)*
Total	104 *(41.6)*	57 *(22.8)*	32 *(12.8)*	33 *(13.2)*	24 *(9.6)*	250 *(100)*
Block - Anthiyur (2)						
Marginal Farmers	24 *(29.3)*	37 *(45.1)*	7 *(8.5)*	8 *(9.8)*	6 *(7.3)*	82*(100)*
Small Farmers	42 *(32.2)*	34 *(25.9)*	25 *(19.1)*	16 *(12.2)*	14 *(10.6)*	131 *(100)*
Large Farmers	8 *(21.6)*	4 *(10.8)*	9 *(24.3)*	3 *(8.1)*	13 *(35.1)*	37 *(100)*
Total	74 *(29.6)*	75 *(30.0)*	41 *(16.4)*	27 *(10.8)*	33 *(13.2)*	250 *(100)*

Source: Field survey

Out of 250 respondents from Block-1, 104 are illiterates, 57 can 'read and write', 32 have only primary education, 33 completed secondary education, and 24 are degree holders. Contrary to Block-1, out of 250 respondents from Block-2, 74 are illiterates, 75 can 'read and write', 41 have primary education, and 27 completed secondary education and 33 degree holders. The land use classification details of the sample households of the two Blocks surveyed are given in Table 5.20. The land under cultivation by farmers in Block-1 is 600 acres and 1,000 acres in Block2.

Table 5.20: Land Use Classification Details of Sample Households

Block - Gobichettipalayam (1)				
Particulars	**Small Holdings**	**Medium Holdings**	**Large Holdings**	**Total**
Own land	45 *(20.2)*	141 *(62.9)*	38 *(16.9)*	224 *(100)*
Leased in	10 *(41.7)*	12 *(49.9)*	2 *(8.3)*	24 *(100)*
Leased out	2 *(100)*	--	--	2 *(100)*
Total	57 *(22.8)*	153 *(61.2)*	40 *(16)*	250 *(100)*
Block - Anthiyur (2)				
Own land	73 *(33.5)*	130 *(59.6)*	15 *(6.9)*	218 *(100)*
Leased in	17 *(53.1)*	15 *(46.9)*	--	32 *(100)*
Leased out	--	--	--	--
Total	90 *(36)*	145 *(58)*	15 *(6.0)*	250 *(100)*

Source: Field Survey.

The table 5.20 shows that in Block-1, out of 250 samples, 153 have own land with majority holding between 4-8 acres of land, and 12 have leased land, of less than two acres. In Block-2, out of 250 sample households, 90 have less than 3 acres, 145 have between 4-8 acres and 15 households have more than 9 acres of land for cultivation. Evidently, the majority of farmers have own land in both the Blocks.

The bases of irrigation in the two Blocks are open wells, rainfall, and bore wells and other sources. In Table 5.21, it is evident that open wells (especially with electrical motors) are the dominant source of irrigation. Rainfall is usually moderate and grossly provides irrigation facilities to the Blocks. In Block-1, open wells have been one of the single largest suppliers of water. Most of them are old wells dug about 25 years ago. No serious effort was made to improve the irrigation facilities by the farmers in the Block but now they are focusing on bore wells. In Block-2 majority of the wells are newly constructed within three years of span. In two Blocks open wells are the single largest providers of irrigation to and bore wells and canal irrigation come next. The most severe problems of farmers related to irrigation are the growing difficulties of accessing sufficient groundwater, the high costs associated with reliance on wells, the tendency towards over-exploitation of groundwater through bore wells preventing sufficient recharge and results existing wells to go dry.

Table 5.21: Irrigation Sources of Sample Households

Particulars	Block - Gobichettipalayam (1)				Block - Anthiyur (2)			
	Open well	**Bore well**	**Other sources**	**Total**	**Open well**	**Bore well**	**Other sources**	**Total**
Marginal farmers	38 *(44.7)*	25 *(29.4)*	22 *(25.8)*	85 *(100)*	51 *(62.2)*	12 *(14.6)*	19 *(23.2)*	82 *(100)*
Small farmers	83 *(70.9)*	21 *(17.9)*	13 *(11.2)*	117 *(100)*	82 *(62.6)*	33 *(25.1)*	16 *(12.2)*	131 *(100)*
Large farmers	29 *(60.4)*	14 *(29.2)*	5 *(10.4)*	48 *(100)*	18 *(48.6)*	12 *(32.4)*	7 *(18.9)*	37 *(100)*
Total	150 *(60.0)*	60 *(24.0)*	40 *(16.0)*	250 *(100)*	151 *(60.4)*	57 *(22.8)*	42 *(16.8)*	250 *(100)*

Source: Field Survey.

The credit sources are broadly categorised as institutional credit and non-institutional credit. In Block-1 most of the farmers are dependent on the non-institutional credit sources, i.e., agricultural moneylenders, professional moneylenders, merchants, traders, friends, relatives and others. They all are locally reachable. In Block-2, the farmers are getting credit from the institutional sources. The credit supplying bank is SBI, located at Gobichettipalayam town. The bank provides loans to the farmers such as, crop loans, gold loans and land mortgage loans. Among the institutions, there exists a uniform rate of interest on direct long-term and short-term agricultural loans to all borrowers.

Table 5.22: Credit Source of Sample Households

Particulars	Block - Gobichettipalayam (1)				Block - Anthiyur (2)			
	Formal loans	**Informal loans**	**Both loans**	**Total**	**Formal loans**	**Informal loans**	**Both loans**	**Total**
Marginal Farmers	28 *(32.9)*	57 *(67.1)*	--	85 *(100)*	30 *(36.6)*	52 *(63.4)*	--	82 *(100)*
Small Farmers	24 *(20.5)*	86 *(73.5)*	7 (6.0)	117 *(100)*	96 *(73.2)*	35 *(26.8)*	--	131 *(100)*
Large Farmers	29 *(60.4)*	7 *(14.6)*	12 *(25.0)*	48 *(100)*	25 (67.5)	7 *(19.0)*	5 *(13.5)*	37 *(100)*
Total	81 *(32.4)*	150 *(60.0)*	19 *(7.6)*	250 *(100)*	151 *(60.4)*	94 *(37.6)*	5 *(2.0)*	250 *(100)*

Source: Field Survey

In Table-5.22, the credit sources of sample households are presented. In Block-1, out of 250 households, 150 households got credit from informal agency, 81 households got credit from the formal agency and 19 households got credit from the both formal and informal agencies. In Block-1, 28 households are marginal farmers, 24 households are small farmers and 29 households are large farmers. In Block-2, among the 250 sample households, 30 households are marginal farmers, 96 households are small farmers and 25 households are large farmers. These households get credit from the bank.

5.9. Determinants of Supply of Agricultural Credit

Institutional Credit performs a noteworthy function in supporting modern production technologies and private investments on the farms by facilitating sufficient amount for the agriculture sector of India even for many developing countries where the majority population depends on agriculture, flow of funds is cyclical and income and savings of the farmers are low. However, it also acts like a double-edged weapon; if used productively it raises productivity and production, but if used irrationally on unproductive activities, it leads to the problem of indebtedness. Several studies have shown that institutional credit has contributed positively to the adoption of modern production inputs and private investments in tube well irrigation, tractorization and other farm machineries, which has contributed towards the growth of the agriculture sector.[1] During the credit sanction process, the borrower is denied access to institutional credit regardless of whether or not he or she has fulfilled the predetermined terms and conditions. In some cases, the farmer is capable to use, but not as much as he or she wants or needs. The main intention of this chapter is to study about dissimilarity in the access to credit and what makes some farm households to reach formal credit and others not. This part also touches on the variations in the credit flow to the borrower.

5.10. Directed Credit and Agriculture Sector

Directed Agricultural Credit system assumes that all farm households would have a positive demand for formal credit and it is a cheaper source for borrowing. It is further assumed that both revealed and potential demand for credit far exceeds the supply. On the basis of this assumption, many countries and financial institutions rely on supply-led approach to extend their credit facility. Irrespective of this approach, most theoretical and empirical studies argue that demand far outweighs the supply of credit. This leads to a situation where banks are compelled to adopt wide scale credit rationing.[2]

Institutional credit is supplied in the form of production credit and investment credit to the farming sector for incurring expenditure on, variable production inputs like fertilizers, seeds, agro-chemicals, labour hiring, machinery hiring, fuel and oil, electric motor charges, etc., private capital formation such as irrigation facility, tractors and other machinery, land development, etc.

Equity issues involved in institutional agricultural credit are widely debated across India. Various farm level studies have shown that the access to institutional finance of smallholders is limited and inadequate.[3] They are excluded from the institutional credit delivery system due to

[1]Vaidyanathan (2005), *"Report of the Task Force on Revival of Rural Cooperative Credit Institutions"*, Ministry of Finance, Government of India, New Delhi.

[2]Sahu and Rajasekhar (2005), "Banking Sector Reform and Credit Flow to Indian Agriculture" *Economic and Political Weekly*, December, pp. *50-59*.

[3]Vyas V.S (2006), "Agrarian Distress: Strategies to Protect Vulnerable Sections", *The Indian Journal of Labour Economics*, 48, 1, January-March.

high transaction cost, poor recovery and low margins. It is proved that the size-wise distribution of agricultural credit to farmers is quite considerable for different farm classes while sharing the amount.

5.11. Ordinary Least Squares Regression Analysis

This section is discusses the variables determining the institutional credit access of the rural farmers. The access of formal credit of farmers is influenced by Percentage of Irrigated area to total area, caste, educational qualification, Income from other than farm resources, Agriculture Workers to Family members, Total Operated Land in Acres, Expenses on Farm Inputs (Includes Fertilizers etc.,), Value of Farm Output, Family Size and Amount of credit given to farmers are tested with the help of Regression Analysis. The test aims at finding out whether the independent variables ($X1$, X_2, X_3.....X_9) do actually have any significant influence on the dependent variable (Y). As SPSS Computer Package for estimating regression model is available, there is no need to go in to the details of computations involved. Regression analysis is used to make prediction about the level and type of association exists between two variables. Simple or Multiple regression analysis is a statistical technique that uses information about the relationship between one or more independent variables and a dependent variable.

The OLS model of the micro level analysis specifies the factors that determine the amount of credit given to the farmer borrower by the commercial banks. The easiest way to analyse the relationships is to examine the regression coefficients for each independent variable. These coefficients still describe the average amount of change to be expected in Y given a unit change in the value of the particular independent variable. Moreover, each particular regression coefficient describes the strength of the relationship between an individual independent variables and the dependent variable. Regression analysis involves estimating an equation, which is usually a linear one and independent variables are considered to be statistically independent. It is well known that multi-collinearity does not exist in case of large samples[1].

The Multiple Linear Equation is:

$$Y = a + b_1X_{1i} + b_2X_{2i} + b_3X_{3i} + b_4X_{4i} + b_5X_{5i} + b_6X_{6i} + b_7X_{7i} + b_8X_{8i} + b_9X_{9i} + u$$

Where Y = Amount of credit given to farmers in rupees

X_1 = Percentage of Irrigated area to total area

X_2 = Backward Caste=1; Others = 0

[1]Srivastava, Shenoy, and Sharma, *(1997), "Quantitative Techniques for Managerial Decisions"*, New Delhi: New Age International, p. 345.

X_3 = Education Above 10th =1, Others = 0

X_4 = Income from other than farm resources

X_5 = Agriculture Workers to Family members

X_6 = Total Operated Land in Acres

X_7 = Expenses on Farm Inputs (Includes Fertilizers etc.,)

X_8 = Value of Farm Output

X_9 = Family Size

a = Regression constant

u = Error term and

$b_1, b_2, b_3....b_9$ = Regression coefficients of independent variables

With the addition of more than one independent variable, a couple of new issues have to be considered. One concern was the possibility that each independent variable may be measured using a different scale. When multiple independent variables were measured with different scales, it was not possible to make relative comparisons between regression coefficients to see which independent variable has the most influence on the dependent variable.

Multiple regression analysis is the most appropriate technique to examine the combined influence of several independent variables on one dependent variable of interest. Multiple independent variables were entered into the same regression equation, and for each variable, a separate regression coefficient was calculated that describes its relationship with the dependent variable. These coefficients examine the relative influence of each independent variable and dependent variable. The type of relationship that exists between each independent variable and dependent measure was still linear. However, with the addition of multiple independent variables, one should think of multiple independent dimensions instead of just a straight-line description.

The results of a regression model were tested to examine its significance include the R^2; the model F statistic; the individual regression coefficients for each independent variable; their associate 't' statistics; and the individual beta coefficients. The appropriate procedure to follow in evaluating the results of a regression analysis was as follows: 1) assess the statistical significance of the overall regression model using the F statistic and its associated probability; 2) evaluate the obtained R^2 to see how large it is; 3) examine the individual regression coefficient to assess relative influence.

Coefficient of determination (R^2) describes the strength of the relationships between all the independent variables in the equation and the dependent variable. It was a measure of the amount of variation in the dependent variable associated with (explained by) the variation in the independent variable. Higher values for R^2 mean stronger relationship between the group of independent variables and the dependent measure. Hence, regression analysis was used to examine the relationship between satisfaction score of the respondents and independent variables such as age, gender, marital status, educational qualification, occupation, account with other banks, and number of years of account operation, frequency of visit and total awareness of respondents.

Table 5.23: Description, Measurement of Variables and Expected Sign

Variable	Description	Expected Sign	All Farmers	Marginal & Small Farmers	Large Farmers
			Mean	Mean	Mean
AC (Y)	Amount of credit given to farmers in rupees	+	58265	32437	86580
PIAGCA (X_1)	Percentage age of Irrigated area to total area	+	26.85	26.34	34.67
CASTE (X_2)	Backward Caste =1; Others = 0	+	0.70	0.64	0.96
EDU (X_3)	Education Above 10th =1	+	0.27	0.21	0.61
OSI (X_4)	Income from other than farm resources	+	10708	7665	25569
AWFM (X_5)	Agriculture Workers to Family members	-	0.47	0.49	0.39
TOL (X_6)	Total Operated Land in Acres	+	4.94	3.56	11.71
EXFIP (X_7)	Expenses on Farm Inputs (Includes Fertilizers etc.,)	+	11898	9650	22876
VAO (X_8)	Value of Farm Output	+	65603	45787	162356
FS (X_9)	Family Size	-	5.24	5.65	3.24
Total			**232**	**178**	**54**

The mean level, expected sign and description of variables for each of the group of farmers are presented in the above Table 5.23. It shows the high the amount of agricultural credit is obtained by large farmers. The table shows that the average of irrigated area to total is also occupied by large farmers; it shows the financial soundness. 70 percentage of the total sample is occupied by backward class. In the case of marginal and small farmers sample, educational level 0.21 out of 1 which clearly shows their illiteracy. Income from other than farm is also important criteria of economic freedom; the average income level is more than ten thousand per year. Higher level of agricultural workers to family members is occupied in the group of small and large farmers. Moreover, they are educationally also at the lower strata. Total Operated Land in Acres is an important factor for classification of farmers, on an average close to 4 acres is the land holdings of Marginal & Small Farmers. Expenses on Farm Inputs (Includes Fertilizers etc.,) are intertwined with demand for credit and farm output as well. Higher the level of farm outputs in terms of value is posted by large farmers group. Regarding the family size, Marginal & Small Farmers households are more which is comparatively higher than the other two groups.

Table 5.24: OLS Regression Estimates for the Selected Sample

Variables	All Farmers (*AF*)		Marginal & Small Farmers (*MSF*)		Large Farmers (*LF*)	
	Coefficient	(t value)	Coefficient	(t-value)	Coefficient	(t-value)
Constant	154.45	8.27**	378. 14	12.38**	1683.31	21.38**
PIAGCA	47. 548	2.66**	0. 225	-9.78**	74. 15	17.76**
CASTE	35.954	1.89	0.365	1.22	58.69	12.74**
EDU	3.166	11.17**	1.13	4.65**	3.20	9.86**
OSI	0. 702	1.32	0.01	7.05**	0. 0 1	15.02**
AWFM	- 1.291	2.54**	-5.27	-10.06**	2.09	9.763**
TOL	- 19.7	7.34**	- 1.04	2.89**	-14. 91	14.45**
EXFIP	0.864	6.78**	1. 87	1.91	0.68	6.90**
VAO	0.072	1.65	0.41	7.13**	0. 06	10.55**
FS	2.13	0.87	1.20	3.65**	0.98	0.06
Adj R^2	0.61		0.56		0.72	
Total Observations	232		178		54	

**significant at 1 percentage level

From the above table, it is observed that the most of the variables have the expected sign and are significant. The coefficient of all farmers PIAGCA is positive and significant at one percentage level, which involves that a unit (one percentage) increases in proportion of irrigated area to gross cropped area, on an average, leads to an increase of 47.54 rupees in the amount of credit (for the entire sample). But in the case of Marginal & Small Farmers sample group it shows very less effect which comparatively scanty than the other two group of sample farmers. The beta value of large farmers is positive and significant at one percentage level, which involves that a unit (one percentage) increases in proportion of irrigated area to gross cropped area, on an average, leads to an increase of 74.15 rupees in the amount of credit. This clearly shows that the positive association between proportions of irrigated area to gross cropped area and access to institutional credit. From the beta value of caste it is found that there is a statistically insignificant relationship exists between amount of institutional credit and caste status. With regard to large farmers, caste status plays a role as a boosting factor to access institutional credit from the banks.

The positive and significant coefficient of Education variable (EDU) clearly shows that the farmers who have possessed 10th standard level of education and above have obtained more credit compared to their less educated counterparts. This variable also behaves in similar direction to marginal and small, and medium and large group of farmers. Income from other sources have less effect in obtaining institutional credit from the banks, is identical to all groups of farmers. The coefficient of worker to family members (WFM) was negative and significant for marginal and small farmers. This indicates that increase in WFM could lead to the less supply of formal credit. The beta value of worker to family members (WFM) was positive and significant for large farmers. This indicates that increase in WFM could lead to the more supply of more credit. Bankers might have perceived that the increase in the number of working members could provide more income through wage or any other economic activity (either farm or non-farm). The beta value of total operated land (TOI) was negative and significant for all groups of farmers. This indicates that increase in TOI could lead to the less supply of institutional credit. Bankers might have perceived that the increase in land holding will not make any sense in income generation after certain point. Probably, this might enhance their creditworthiness.

5.12. Conclusion

This section has employed ordinary least square regression to find out the determinants of supply of agricultural credit at household level. From the results it is found that the determinants of access to formal credit are influenced by several factors. The farm, and household characteristics such as quality of land, value of assets excluding land which is often used as a collateral, irrigated area, and educational qualification of the borrower determines the access to formal credit in a vibrant way. It is quite interesting to note that the quality of land and value of output are found to be significant in determining the access to formal credit and the amount obtained respectively, rather than the size of landholding. It appears that, the mere existence of formal credit institutions does not guarantee that marginal and small farmers will benefit from them. This is inevitable that the cultivation and the credit system are interdependent on one on another. Agriculture is an unorganized sector where credit influences factors of production. Credit through formal institutions would help farmers to buy better inputs such as high yielding variety seeds (HYVs), fertilizers, pesticides, labour force, modern technology, etc. The availability of credit with lower interest rates would enable farmers to invest more money on land for improving the productivity of the land.

CHAPTER VI

A SUMMARY OF FINDINGS, SUGGESTIONS AND CONCLUSION

6.1. Introduction

This study aims to work on the quantitative importance of commercial bank credit to agriculture not only at a macroeconomic level but also includes the relevant institutions such as banks and the ultimate farmers possibly interactions between them. This study intends to give a better insight into the relative quantitative impact of changes in bank credit in emerging economy like India where the Directed Credit policy prevails. The programmes of directed credit attempt to intervene in the way that banks allocate credit. Without government intervention, the bank will not allocate funds to those projects for which the social returns are the highest. This is true even in the absence of technological spillovers. But these are benefits that conventional banking might simply ignore. By the same token, the widespread problems many banks faced when real estate markets collapsed provide strong evidence that financial institutions failed to take social returns into account in making real estate loans. Directed credit-this time, restrictions on certain categories of loans may be desirable. This chapter summarises the findings and conclusions of the study and offer suggestions for betterment of policy framework.

6.1.1. Objectives

In light of these issues, the present study on credit flow to agriculture derives its relevance and has the following objectives.

- To study the trends of agricultural credit by commercial banks before and after the introduction of the banking sector reforms;
- To study the effect of Macro level variables on agricultural credit by commercial banks;
- To analyse the effect of Bank level variables on agricultural credit by commercial banks and
- To examine the effect of Micro level variables on agricultural credit by commercial banks

6.1.2. Hypotheses

The following hypotheses are tested in relation to the above objectives.

- The agricultural credit by commercial banks may not differ with Macro level variables

- There is no significant difference between bank level characteristics and agricultural credit by commercial banks.
- There is no significant difference between Micro level characteristics and agricultural credit by commercial banks.

6.1.3. *Methodology*

The validity of any research is based on the systematic method of data collection and analysis. Both secondary and primary data were used for the present study. The secondary data were collected from authenticated publications. The primary data were collected from 500 respondents from Gobichettipalayam and Anthiyur blocks of Erode District.

6.1.4. *Sources of Secondary Data*

The data required for the study was taken from the various reports of Reserve Bank of India (RBI) and NABARD. The macro level variables and Bank level variables were collected from the annual reports of RBI, Handbook of Statistics on Indian Economy and Report on Currency and Finance. The macro level variables covered the years from 1971 to 2011. In order to evaluate the impact econometrically, there was a problem of paucity of observations. This said problem has been overcome by using the data, since 1971. This even precise the estimation and the results are robust in nature without any degree of freedom problem. The bank level variables pertaining to the period from 2001 to 2010 were included. The unbalanced panel data set based on annual data is developed for 27 banks and utilised with panel analysis for bank level variables.

The micro level variables pertaining to Tamil Nadu were taken through Situation Assessment Survey of Farmers Indebtedness of Farmer Households: NSS 59th Round (January–December 2003). The credit related data of Erode District were collected from the Annual Credit Plan of the Erode district from 2006-2011 with the intention to get better understanding of the study area.

6.1.5. *Sources of Primary Data*

The researcher has chosen State Bank of India in Erode District for the purpose of this study. The present study has used the length of canal used for irrigation as a proxy variable to identify the advanced and backward blocks[1]. The blocks namely Gobichettipalayam (from advanced group) and Anthiyur (backward group) were selected randomly. Further, SBI

[1]There is a tendency for formal credit to flow towards agriculturally more developed regions and to relatively larger farmers, leaving the backward regions and small farmers to the informal market.

Gobichettipalayam branch of Gobichettipalayam Block and SBI Anthiyur branch of Anthiyur block (falling within the service area of these bank branches) were purposively selected.

With a view to give representation to different categories of farmers, 500 farmers who belong to the area of operation of SBI Gobichettipalayam and Anthiyur branch, and who have exclusively borrowed from the SBI, were selected for the study. While selecting the sample, care was taken to include the farmers who have not made any other investment previously, That is, the farmers who wanted the finance from the bank and made investment only in the agriculture were selected. The farmers who have availed finance one year before the study period was selected and farmers who were at the doorsteps of the bank for loan were also included. Representation was given to different categories of farmers like marginal, small and other categories of farmers.

6.1.6. Sampling Scheme

The main sketch of this study is to examine the formal credit for agricultural sector in India with specific reference to two blocks of Erode district of Tamil Nadu. The proportional study between the two blocks of Erode district were selected where the area of operation of SBI and who have exclusively borrowed from the SBI branch to understand and review institutional credit at village level. The overall purpose of the work is to find how credit was rationed to the different category of farmers.

6.1.7. Selection of Sample Farmers and Collection of Data

Purposive sampling method was adopted for the selection of farmers from the State bank of India branch of Gobichettipalayam and Anthiyur. The farmers, who visited the Gobichettipalayam and Anthiyur branches during the period between August 2010 and December 2010, were considered as targeted population of sample farmers. A well-structured interview schedule in English was prepared and 550 bank customers of two branches in the ratio of 1:1 were interviewed. The residential addresses of sample farmers with mobile numbers were collected. Based on that the customers were interviewed and required data were collected from the sample farmers. On an average one hour has required to interview a farmer. Out of 550 sample farmers interviewed, 505 interview schedules were finalised. Owing to inconsistency, 500 sample farmers were considered for final analysis.

6.1.8. Field Work and Collection of Data

Before the data collection, a model interview schedule was used for the purpose of pilot study. The schedule was pre-tested with the response obtained from 70 farmers. The feedback of the respondents was useful in carrying out a few corrections/ modifications in the questions included earlier schedule.

6.2. Findings of the Study

Macro Level Variables and Agriculture Credit by Commercial Banks (III Chapter)

Block Causality over the Selected Macro Level Variables

It was apparent that the block causality relationship between macroeconomic and agricultural performance variables was examined. The causality analysis is carried out within the framework of 'block causality' of variables in the VAR. The 'Granger Block Causality' tests allow an assessment of the strength of the transmission mechanisms. A variable x is said to Granger cause a variable y if past values of x are useful for predicting values of y. Rejection of H_0 through the standard F-test attests to the inclusion of a particular variable in the inclusion of another variable.

It was found that the evidence of block causality from macro level characteristics to direct agricultural credit shows strong relationship. This is even more acute, when we omit CRR from the group. Here, the null hypothesis which carries no relationship between macro characteristics to DFA is rejected at one percentage level of significance. The block causality from the macro level variables to IDF appears as insignificant when we included the whole group of variables. By analysing the individual granger cause the RCB has omitted and there is a significant relationship with this subset.

Impulse Response of Direct Finance to Agriculture over the Selected Variables

It was evident that the positive impact of rise in ADL throughout the period suggests that the agriculture sector benefits from the saving habit of the masses. The positive impact of AGDP is for initial two years and up to 10 years it shows negative impact which shows capital formation may not act as substitute by direct finance to agriculture. The reason behind this is that government is reluctant in giving importance to agriculture as compared to industry. Even the minimum supportive price announced by the government, sometimes may not cover the input made by the farmers. The influence of middlemen, monsoon failure, seasonal nature of the product, poor storage facilities are factors which limit the share of agriculture in GDP. The study observe that the increase in CRR shows initially the positive response with the direct credit to agriculture but after 2 years it consistently negative in providing credit towards agriculture. It was visible that the Co-operative and regional rural banks take a lead in providing agricultural credit and only in later stage there is increasing share of DFA by commercial banks and shift has moved from co-operative to commercial banking in catering the needs of the agricultural sector. Investment in statutory securities is one of the methods of the government in restraining credit supply. But even at the point of view of the banker, it is safer to invest in government securities. RCB variable shows the number of rural branches to total bank branches in India. When, the higher the number of rural branches results in increasing focus on direct finance to agriculture.

Impulse Response of Indirect Finance to Agriculture over the Selected Variables

It was located that the positive impact of rise in ADL throughout the period suggests that the agriculture sector benefits from the saving habit of the masses. The above result clearly tells about the positive shock of aggregate level deposits to indirect finance to agriculture. The negative impact of AGDP is for initial three years which reveals that there is lack of effect in that short term period.

It was disclosed that there is a positive impact of indirect credit flow to agriculture on the tenth year onwards shows that the growth always fuels the credit delivery and vice versa. It is observed that the impulses are uniformly negative for the CRR throughout the period. CRR is considered as one of the important policy channel of the central bank in India. It clearly indicated that there is an immediate and consistent long term negative relationship between CRR and indirect finance to agriculture. The general hypothesis is that Higher the credit provided by CRRBL (Co-operative and Regional Rural Banks) shows lower the commercial bank credit because Co-operative societies and Regional Rural Banks are considered as one of the substituted institutional framework to focus on agriculture alone.

Bank Level Variables and Agriculture Credit by Commercial Banks (IV Chapter)

The role of commercial banks has occupied a new meaning and significance, in view of the changing structure and requirements of a developing economy. The increased horizon of commercial banks identifies itself with the problems and responsibilities for making banking an instrument for bringing about the social and economic transformation of a developing country. Banks have become the prime movers and pace setters for the achievement of socio-economic objectives of the country.

The present financial system in India is large with a variety of banks, financial institutions, capital market institutions, non-banking institution and a number of indigenous banks. Among the financial institutions in India, banks are prominent financial intermediaries and in fact, financial inter-mediation is largely synonymous with banking.

Base Line Panel data estimates for Bank Characteristics and Credit Flow to Agriculture

From the base line model it was found that the ROA is the profitability of the bank having positive relationship with the credit to agriculture in a significant way. This gives support to the argument that lending increases with profitability of commercial banks. This is consistent with the existing argument that the profitability is generally positively correlated with bank lending. SIZE of the bank also has positive relationship with the credit to agriculture. This confirms the argument that big size banks are less prone to financial distress. This also suggests that commercial banks lend more if they have greater ability to absorb adverse shocks by way of loan defaults and big Size.

The cost of funds (COF) and risk level (VOL) are having the negatively significant relationship with the credit to agriculture. This leads to the argument that the excess cost of fund may be the credit to different sector especially directed credit. If firms are not stable in their earnings capacity, risky loans are not avoided but postponed in the case of directed credit.

Sector wise Panel Data Estimates for Bank Level Variables and Credit Flow to Agriculture

From the sector wise panel data estimates, it was observed that The ROA is the profitability of the bank having positive relationship with the credit to agriculture to all the selected sectors except for private banks in a significant way. This gives support to the argument that lending increases with profitability of commercial banks but this might not worked in the case of private banks. This was consistent with the existing argument that the profitability is generally positively correlated with bank lending but private banks may have more avenues to invest in a fruitful way than the agriculture sector. SIZE of the bank also has positive relationship with the credit to agriculture.

The cost of funds (COF) shows negatively significant relationship with the credit flow to agriculture by private banks and nationalized banks and strength of impact of COF on agriculture credit is comparatively lower for nationalized banks. The relationship between COF and credit flow to agriculture for the SBI & Associates are statistically in significant. Risk level (VOL) is having the negatively significant relationship with the credit to agriculture both for private banks and for nationalized banks. If firms are not stable in their earnings capacity, risky loans are not avoided but postponed in the case of directed credit. There is a insignificant relationship between VOL and credit flow to agriculture for SBI & its associates.

Capital adequacy norms (CAR) shows statistically significant relationship with the private sector banks and it shows insignificant relationship with the nationalized and SBI & its associates. The non performing assets ratio shows negative relationship with the credit to agriculture and it is significant in the case of Nationalised banks. Negative relationship confirms that banks reacting negatively towards ouverdues but government may also stress some basic outlay to the agriculture. The coefficient of variation adjusted R^2 of private sector banks is quite high of 46.6 percentage which is comparatively higher than the remaining two sectors of banks which are also in the field of agriculture credit.

Micro Level Variables and Agriculture Credit by Commercial Banks (V Chapter)

Multiple regression analysis is the most appropriate technique to examine the combined influence of several independent variables on one dependent variable of interest. Multiple independent variables were entered into the same regression equation, and for each variable, a separate regression coefficient was calculated that describes its relationship with the dependent variable. These coefficients examine the relative influence of each independent variable and dependent variable. The type of relationship that exists between each independent variable and dependent measure was still linear. However, with the addition of multiple independent variables, one should think of multiple independent dimensions instead of just a straight-line description.

It was observed that the most of the variables have the expected sign and are significant. The coefficient of all farmers PIAGCA is positive and significant at one percentage level, which involves that a unit (one percentage) increases in proportion of irrigated area to gross cropped area, on an average, leads to an increase of 47.54 rupees in the amount of credit (for the entire sample).

But in the case of Marginal & Small Farmers sample group it shows very less effect which comparatively scanty than the other two group of sample farmers. The beta value of large farmers is positive and significant at one percentage level, which involves that a unit (one percentage) increases in proportion of irrigated area to gross cropped area, on an average, leads to an increase of 74.15 rupees in the amount of credit. This clearly shows that the positive association between proportions of irrigated area to gross cropped area and access to institutional credit. From the beta value of caste it is found that there is a statistically in significant relationship exists between amount of institutional credit and caste status. With regard to large farmers, caste status plays a role as a boosting factor to access institutional credit from the banks.

6.3. Suggestions

6.3.1. Research Based Suggestions

A. Analysis of Block Causality on Macro Variables

- Since, the evidence of block causality from macro level variables to direct agricultural credit shows strong relationship and cause is proved. Hence, it is suggested that macro level mismanagement should be avoided to insulate agriculture from external shocks.
- From the Granger block causality tests, this was used to find out the relationship between aggregate level and indirect credit and total credit to agriculture also significant. This suggests that agriculture sector should insulate from the macro level changes.
- From the cause result, rural commercial bank branches acting as an important contributor for the direct credit flow to agriculture. Hence, it is suggested rural banking network is one of the major factor in driving the credit to the agriculture sector.

B. Analysis of Impulse Response of Direct Finance to Agriculture

- The positive impact of AGDP is for initial two years and for the rest, up to 10 years it shows negative impact which shows capital formation may not act as substitute by direct finance to agriculture. So, it is suggested that government should not consider agriculture as a profit making industry but to take it as a livelihood for millions of poor in framing the development schemes.
- The study observed that the increase in cash reserves shows the positive response with the direct credit to agriculture for initial two years. But after two years, it was consistently negative in providing credit towards agriculture. Therefore, it is suggested that the government should stick on the provision for the directed credit towards the priority sector.
- The positive result between cooperatives and regional rural banks and credit to agriculture clearly suggests that strengthening of cooperative and regional rural banks are necessary for the flow to credit to agriculture which may substitute the rural commercial bank branches.
- RCB variable shows the number of rural branches to total bank branches in India. When, the higher the number of rural branches results in increasing focus on direct finance to agriculture. So it is suggested that rural branches that specific focus on agriculture is necessary.

C. *Analysis of Impulse Response of Indirect Finance to Agriculture*

- RCB means shows the number of rural branches to total bank branches in India. There is a quiet interesting negative relationship between rural branches and indirect finance to agriculture. The nature of the indirect finance to agriculture is different from the direct finance to agriculture. Hence, it is suggested that the indirect finance to agriculture should not be parallel with the direct finance to agriculture.
- It clearly indicated that there is an immediate and consistent long term negative relationship between CRR and indirect finance to agriculture. Thus, it is suggested that credit squeeze is definite, out of increasing cash reserve for banking system.

D. *Analysis of Bank Level Variables and Credit Flow to Agriculture*

- The profitability of the bank is having positive relationship with the credit to agriculture to all the selected sectors except for private banks in a significant way. This gives support to the argument that lending increases with profitability of commercial banks but this might not worked in the case of private banks. Here, it is suggested that private banks are monitored with the mandated lending towards agriculture.
- The cost of funds (COF) shows negatively significant relationship with the credit flow to agriculture by private banks and nationalized banks and strength of impact of COF on agriculture credit is comparatively lower for nationalized banks. The relationship between COF and credit flow to agriculture for the SBI & Associates are statistically insignificant. Hence, it is suggested that bank level agriculture credit portfolios should be checked by an autonomous committee.
- Capital Adequacy Ratio (CAR) shows statistically significant relationship with the private sector banks and it shows insignificant relationship with the nationalized and SBI & its Associates. For this reason, it is advocated that capital adequacy should not be waived but gradually implemented in the banking system. Otherwise, it will reduce the priority credit to the different sectors of the economy.
- The non performing assets ratio shows negative relationship with the credit to agriculture and it is significant in the case of Nationalised banks. Negative relationship confirms that banks are reacting negatively towards overdue. Hence, it is recommended that government may also stress some basic outlay to the agriculture through bailout packages.

E. *Analysis of Micro Level Variables and Credit Flow to Agriculture*

- It is clearly apparent about the source of loan agencies including the banks. It is apparent from the table that majority of the farmers in Tamil Nadu are depending on Block/agricultural professional money lenders for their financial requirement irrespective of the different land class holdings. Especially, the land size class (A)1, were that higher the numbers of farmers, still depending on Block money lenders for their financial requirement. Hence, it is suggested that credit should be directed towards marginal and small farmers.
- This finding also substantiated by the task force in other way that, the share of cooperatives in the total outstanding debt of farmers was only 19.6%. However, in the five states of Gujarat, Haryana Kerala, Maharashtra and Tamil Nadu, cooperative credit societies were an important source of credit (shares being in the range of 23-49%). However, as in some cases the credit lines were choked they could be reflecting old rather than current year loans.2 Hence, it is suggested that credit should be reimbursed based on genuine circumstance.
- It is found from the block level data out of 250 households, 150 households got credit from informal agency, 81 households got credit from the formal agency and 19 households got credit from the both of formal and informal agencies are shown. Hence, it is recommended that credit need to properly rationed.
- It is clear that the positive and significant coefficient of Education variable (EDU) clearly shows that the farmers who have possessed a 10th standard level of education and above have obtained more credit compared to their less educated counterparts. This variable also behaves in similar direction to marginal and small, and medium and large group of farmers. So, it is advocated that illiterate should not be discriminated and there should be a sub class of preference for illiterates.
- It is discovered that the beta value of total operated land (TOI) was negative and significant for all groups of farmers. This indicates that increase in TOI could lead to the less supply of institutional credit. Bankers might have perceived that the increase in land holding will not make any sense in income generation after certain point. Thus, it is suggested that bankers should focus on per capita credit for operating land.

---

[1]Size of land < 0.01 hectare.

[2]GOI (2010), Ministry of Agriculture, *Report of the Task Force on Credit Related Issues of Farmers*, June, pp.28.

6.3.2. General Suggestions

- Out of 500 respondents who represent different classes of farmers, majority of them have expressed their dissatisfaction for not conducting periodical meet by the bank. It is the need to educate the farmers on the various aspects of banking. Efforts should be made to encourage large number of farmers to avail the exclusive services provided by the banks such as Kisan credit card scheme (KCC), National Agricultural Development Programme (NADP), Subsidy schemes announced by state governments etc., Survey should be conducted to get the feedback on the level of service received by them and rectification should be made in the areas of dissatisfaction.
- Several farmers have no awareness about the services provided by other governmental agencies for agriculture. Several schemes are proposed by Ministry of water resources, Ministry of Agriculture, Ministry of environment and financed by Ministry of finance through NABARD should be popularised by the local banking network.
- Several respondents of different agriculture groups were highly dissatisfied with bankers for not listening to and finding out a solution to their complaints regarding crop loan. Hence, it is suggested that the complaints of the farmers should be handled promptly and in a systematic manner. The bank staff should listen to the complaints of the farmers patiently to find out a solution.

6.4. Conclusion

The present study was an attempt to ascertain the agricultural credit by commercial banks at Macro and Micro levels.

The study not only highlights on macro level variables on agricultural credit by commercial banks and strongly concluded that the agriculture sector is not insulated from the policy level effects at the macro level. By the very fact, agriculture sector is considered to be the vital sector for several people's livelihood; the drawback should be curbed in economic growth process where banks' roles are inseparable.

The study concludes that there is unequal credit rationing towards the agriculture sector and it made the farm not a profitable business at all. It was therefore earnestly hoped that the authorities will consider the suggestions recommended herewith for improving the issues of farmers in general and agriculture credit in particular.

6.5. Suggestions for Future Research

The following lines of research are suggested for the future researchers on agricultural credit and farmers' issue.

- The influence of awareness of credit schemes in accessing institutional credit.
- Cost-Benefit Analysis of agricultural credit operations of Public Sector Banks and Private sector banks in Erode District.
- Impact of technological innovations on Farmer satisfaction.
- Satisfaction of farmers with regard to debt waiving schemes of Public Sector Banks and Private Sector Banks.
- Application of Credit Risk Models for Directed Lending.

Bibliography

A. *Books*

1. Abrol Prem Nath, "Commercial Banking", New Delhi: Anmol Publication, 1987.
2. B.P. Aggarwal, "Commercial Banking in India", New Delhi, Classical Publishing Company, 1981.
3. I.J. Ahluwalia, "Industrial Growth in India: Stagnation Since the Mid-Sixties", Oxford University Press, New Delhi, 1985.
4. K.M. Ahmed, "Banking in India", New Delhi: Anmol Publications, 1992.
5. Anderson, "Thesis and Assignment Writing", New Delhi: Wiley Eastern Limited, 1970.
6. Aron, "Modernisation of Agriculture in Developing Countries: Resources, Potentials and Problems", Binghamton: John Wiley and Sons, 1981.
7. C.L. Bansal, "Management of Commercial Banks, Financial Markets and Institutions", New Delhi: Hari Anand Publications, 1993.
8. P. Bardhan, "Land, Labour, and Rural Poverty: Essays for Development Economics", Delhi: Oxford University Press, 1984.
9. P.Bardhan, "The Economic Theory of Agrarian Institutions", Oxford: Clarendon Press, 1989.
10. K. Basu, "Rural Credit Markets: The Structure of Interest Rates, Exploitation and Efficiency", In P.K. Bardhan (ed.). The Economic Theory of Agrarian Institutions. Oxford: Clarendon Press, 1989.
11. C. Bell and Srinivasan, "Some Aspects of Linked Products and Credit Market Contracts Among Risk Neutral Agents", In Pranab K Bardhan (ed), The Economic Theory of Agrarian Institutions. Oxford: Oxford University Press.
12. K.C. Chakrabarty, "Banking in 1990", Bombay: Himalayan Publishing House, 1990.
13. A.C. Chawla and Uppal, "Indian Banking Towards 21st Century", New Delhi: Deep and Deep Publications, 1988.
14. K. Deb, "Indian Banking Since Independence", New Delhi: Ashish Publishing House, 1998.
15. S. Gangopadhyay, "Some Issues in Interlinked Agrarian Markets", In Kaushik Basu (ed.), Agrarian Questions. New Delhi: Oxford University Press, 1997.
16. W.H. Greene, "Econometric Analysis", Prentice Hall, New Jersey, USA, 1990.
17. S.B. Gupta, "Monetary Economic Institutions and Policy", New Delhi:S.Chand and Company, 1985.
18. S.P. Gupta, "Statistical Method", New Delhi: Sultan Chand and Sons, 2000.

19. B. Hair and Ortinau, "Marketing Research", New Delhi: Tata McGraw-Hill Publishing Company Limited, 2003.
20. T.R. Jain, "Commercial Banks Meaning and Function", New Delhi; VK Publication, 2001.
21. Jaiswal, "Bank Finance to Corporate Sector in India", New Delhi:Deep and Deep Publication, 1989.
22. Joshi Vijay and Little, "India's Economic Reforms", New Delhi: Oxford University Press, 1996.
23. U. Kapila (Ed), "Indian Economy Since Independence", Academic Foundation, New Delhi, 1998.
24. A. Koutsoyiannis, "Theory of Econometrics", Kundli: Replika Press Private Limited, 2004.
25. K. Krishnamurty and V. Pandit, "Macroeconometric Modeling of the Indian Economy", Hindustan Publishing Company, 1985.
26. P. Krishnamurty and G. Mahanty, "Policies for Stability and Growth Experiments with a Large and Comprehensive Structural Model for India", In Economic Policy Modelling for India, Oxford University Press, New Delhi, 2004.
27. O.R. Krishnasami and Ranganatham, "Methodology of Research in Social Sciences", New Delhi: Himalaya Publishing House, 2007.
28. S. Lalwani, "Changing Profile of Indian Banking", NewDelhi: Radha Publications, 1992.
29. Bhatia, "Cost of Cultivation and Farm Income in India", Department of agriculture and Cooperation, Ministry of Agriculture, (New Delhi, Academic Foundation), 2004.
30. Maheshwari and Paul, "Banking and Financial System", New Delhi: Kalyani Publishers, 1998.
31. Misra, "Banking Sector and Narasimham Committee Recommendations–An Appraisal", New Delhi: Deep and Deep Publications, 1994.
32. Pandit, "The Growth and Structure of Savings in India: An Econometric Analysis", New Delhi: Oxford University Press, 1991.
33. Reddy, "Future of Rural Banking". In Raj Kapila (cd.), India's Banking and Financial Sectors in New Millellinum. New Delhi: Academic Foundation, 2001.
34. Sen and Bhatia, "Cost of Cultivation and Farm Income in India", Department of agriculture and Cooperation, Ministry of Agriculture, (New Delhi, Academic Foundation), 2004.
35. Sen Abhijit , "Agricultural Price Policy: Achievements and the Emerging Problems", in Y V Krishna Rao (ed) New Challenges Facing Indian Agriculture, 1999.
36. Sharma, "The Role of Commercial Banks in India's Developing Economy", New Delhi: S.Chand and Company Ltd, 1974.

37. M. Sooden, "Regional Disparities of Commercial Banking in India", Delhi: Kanishka Publishing House, 1992.
38. Subrahmanya,"Modern Banking in India", New Delhi: Deep & Deep Publications, 1982.
39. Thamarajakshi, "Intersectoral Relationships in a Developing Economy: The Indian Experience", Academic Foundation, 1994.

B. Articles

1. I.J. Ahluwalia and C. Rangarajan, "Agriculture and Industry: A study of Linkages the Indian Experience", Mimeo, World Economic Congress of International Association, 1986.
2. Aryeetey Ernest, "Rural Finance in Africa: Institutional Development and Access the Poor", Annual World Bank Conference on Development Economics, The World Bank, 1996.
3. S. Mahendra Dev and C. Ravi, "Poverty and Inequality: All India and States, 1983-2005", Economic and Political Weekly, Vol. 42, No. 6, Pp. 509-521, 2007.
4. N. Krishnaji, "Agricultural Price Policy: A Survey with Reference to Indian Foodgrain Economy", Economic and Political Weekly, Vol. 25, No. 26, 1990.
5. V.K. Ramachandran and Madhura Swaminathan, "Does Informal Credit Provide Security? Rural Banking Policy in India", Geneva: International Labour Office, 2001.
6. Rangarajan, "Agricultural Growth and Industrial Performance", International Food Policy Research Institute, 1982.
7. Rangarajan, "Rural India, The Role of Credit", Reserve Bank of India Bulletin, Bombay: RBI, 1996.
8. Sarap, "Factors Affecting Small Farmers' Access to Institutional Credit in Rural Orissa, India", Development and Change, Vol. 21, No. 2, Pp. 281-307, 1990.
9. Satyasai and Viswanathan, "Commercialisation and Diversification of Indian Agriculture", Occasional Paper No. 5, National Bank for Agriculture and Rural Development, Mumbai, 1997.
10. Satyasai and Viswanathan, "Dynamics of Agriculture-Industry Linkages", Indian Journal of Agricultural Economics, Vol. 54, No. 3, Pp. 394-401, 1999.
11. Shivamaggi, "Reforms in Rural Banking: Need for Bolder Approach", Economic and Political Weekly, Vol. 35, No. 20, Pp. 1714-18, 2000.
12. M. Singh, "Inaugural Address at the 54th Annual Conference of the Indian Society of Agricultural Economics", Indian Journal of Agricultural Economics, Vol. 50, No. 1, Pp. 1-6, 1995.
13. Storm, "The Macroeconomic Impact of Agricultural Policy: A CGE Analysis for India", Journal of Policy Modeling, Vol. 16, 1994.

C. Reports

1. GOI, "All-India Debt and Investment Survey", Report No. 501, NSS 59th Round, NSSO, MOSPI, New Delhi: Government of India, 2005.
2. GOI, "Report of the Task Force on Credit Related Issues of Farmers" (Chairman: U. C. Sarangi), Submitted to the Ministry of Agriculture, Government of India, June, 2010.
3. Planning Commission, "Approach Paper for the Tenth Five-Year Plan", Government of India, 2000.
4. Reserve Bank of India, "Handbook of Statistics on Indian Economy", 2012.
5. Reserve Bank of India, "Statistical tables relating to banks in India 2007- 2012", Retrieved from http://www.rbi.org.in, 2009.
6. Reserve Bank of India, Report on Trend and Progress of Banking in India, Reserve Bank of India: Mumbai.

D. Electronic Retrievals

1. Economic Growth and Stability: Experiences in Selected Asian and Latin for Indian banks, (2008), Retrieved from http://knowledge.wharton.upenn.edu.
2. Knowledge@wharton (2009, 15th Nov). Raghuram Rajan on Rewriting the rules for Indian banks, Retrieved from http://knowledge.wharton.upenn.edu.
3. PTI (2009, 18th May), 20-PSU Banks Fail to Meet Farm Sector Lending Target till Nov., The economic times, Retrieved from http://economictimes.indiatimes.com
4. Ramasubba (2009), Discriminatory Rural Credit Policy, Retrieved from www.Indian farmers.org

www.ingramcontent.com/pod-product-compliance
Lightning Source LLC
Chambersburg PA
CBHW071346230926
51846CB00002B/463

* 9 7 8 9 3 8 6 6 3 8 3 9 7 *